JOYFUL NOISE

Make a joyful noise unto the Lord.
Psalm 100

This collection is intended as a working tool for people of all ages to join together to make *joyful noises* of fun, fellowship and faith. It is a musical cafeteria of songs for children, young people, women's groups, men's groups, senior citizens, good singers and monotones.

This light-weight, portable volume of songs includes rounds, folksongs, nonsense and motion songs, Christmas music, hymns, spirituals, patriotic and religious songs, both old and new. It has songs to honor, greet and get-acquanted and songs to say good-bye.

TO MAKE IT LEGAL

The royalties for the songs in this book represent more than half the printing cost. If you have enough books to pass around, you have helped pay the royalties. To keep the cost low enough to make it possible for the groups to buy them in sufficient quantity, we're doing this vocal edition non-profit.

This is important to us because all too often church and community groups have violated U.S. copyright law by copying material without permission, feeling that it is all right because , *It's for a good cause* or *They're not being sold, they're for our own use*. But that is no different from stealing someone's peaches for our own use. Legally you can't even project copyrighted words or music on the wall or screen or make up a grace to the tune of *Edelweiss* and issue a song sheet, without permission, unless you omit the music. Permission is the key.

ACKNOWLEDGMENTS

The name of the collection came from the T-shirt of a happy young kid at Will Rogers United Methodist Church in Tulsa, as he joyfully climbed the stairs to make music with his group JOYFUL NOISE; it registered!

Special appreciation to the Will Rogers Church; the pastor, Larry Jacobson; musicians Hugo Garza-Ortiz, John Pryor, Pam Lundy and Susan Lewis.

This collection has its roots in the Eisenberg family life which included singing around the piano with sister Frances playing; Dad's Junior Choir in the twenties at Park City Church in Knoxville, my own experience leading singing and recreation for the 1949 National Conference at Winona Lake, Indiana. From there, I went on to be part of the youth staff of the General Board of Education of the Methodist Church from 1945-52, during which time I often led singing with groups numbering from 5,000 to 10,000. My thanks also to those who provided accompaniment: Joe Bell, Emiline Crane, Hoover Rupert, May Titus and my good wife Helen.

Other groups who have kept singing alive have supported my efforts. We owe a lot to Lynn and Katherine Rohrbough, who with the notation help of Jane Keene, developed custom song books. "Gus" Zanzig also helped community singing with publications like *Singing America.* The list of those who have helped the singing movement by leading or by compiling songs includes Annabeth Brandle, Wally Chappel, Don Clayton, Russell Ames Cook, Gene Durham, E.O. Harbin, Pete Seeger and Janet Tobitt.

Recreation Laboratories, now numbering twenty-eight, promote folk singing as does the American Camping Association. They give opportunities to experiment under the leadership of such people as Jack Pearse, the designated leader of the American Camping Association of Camp Tawingo, Canada; Chris Jesperson, Mary Lib Lowery, Tommy Miller, Charlotte Mosely, Nina Reeves, Fred Smith, Warren Willis and most recently, Chuck Bradley and friends at the Hoosier Lab, Bradford Woods, Indiana.

The inclusion of spirituals stems from the love of them I developed at the feet of John W. Work at Fisk University, the inspired singing of Roland Hayes at the great Cleveland Conference and the irrepressible Julius Scott.

For encourgement and ideas, we thank R. Harold Hipps and his wife Kitten who polled Christian Education professionals and sent detailed suggestions as did John Lundys, Bill Mann and Steve Swecker. Our thanks to Jim Snead for arranging the launching of **JOYFUL NOISE** at the 1989 Purdue Convocation.

Earl Carter, Tom Curtis, Nancy Marsh, Max Marvel, Don and Constance Waddell and the special people at South Central Assembly, Mt. Sequoyah, Fayetteville, Arkansas and the VOLUNTEERS IN MISSION people who let me practice on them.

Susan Wilkie has offered promotional cooperation and Dub Amborose and Tate Newland have made youth song suggestions.

Robin Dreyer has worked on all the details, especially copyright clearance, has set much of the book on the new IBM Musicwriter and has given special counsel over and over again as has his wife, Tammy.

COMPILING AND PRINTING has been in the hands of World Around Songs, the successors of the Rohrboughs who not only pioneered in custom books, but had a marvelous cache of 3,500 songs in the file. Paul Cope, who now owns World Around Songs, went with us to Faith Printing to work out details and is responsible for completing the negatives from which the printing plates are made.

PRINTING is by consultation with Ravenel Scott and David Chastain, Faith Printing Company, 4210 Locust Hill Road, Taylors, SC 29687-8911, with binding at Nicholstone Binders, 418 Harding Industrial Drive, Nashville, TN 37211.

DISTRIBUTION is being handled by World Around Songs, 5790 Highway 80 South, Burnsville, NC 28714.

We recommend them for custom song books, quality printing and binding. We found them to be most reasonable and cooperative.

Any true movement is a singing movement. --Hiel Bollinger.

Sing For the Singing

Sing, sing sing for the singing
The whole day long.
Sing, sing, voices are ringing in heartfelt song.
Sing, sing, whate'er betide you,
Sing for the joy of the spirit inside you.
Sing, the song's the thing!
Sing, sing, loving the singing,
Just sing, sing, sing.

He's Got the Whole World

Spiritual
C
1. He's got the whole world in His hands,
G7
C
He's got the whole world in His hands,
He's got the whole world in His hands,
G7
C
He's got the whole world in His hands

2. He's got the tiny little baby in His hands, (3x)
   He's got the whole world in His hands.
3. He's got you and me, brother, / sister, in His hands...
4. He's got everybody in His hands...

MOTIONS:

1. Standing up, form a big, round world with both hands and arms. On "in His hands" hold out hands, palms up.
2. Rock imaginary baby in arms, then hold out hands, as above.
3. Singing "brother" or "sister", point to appropriate persons close to you, then hold out hands.
4. Swing arms out wide, almost as to hit the people next to you, then hold out hands.

In a Cottage in the Woods

G 1
D7
2
In a cot-tage in the woods, Lit-tle man by the
G
3
C
win-dow stood; Saw a rab-bit hop-ping by,
4 D7
G
5 Spoken
Fright-ened as can be. "Help me! Help me!
D7
6
G
Help," he cried, "'Ere the hun-ter shoot me dead!"
7
C
8 D7
G
"Lit-tle rab-bit, come in-side, Safe-ly to a-bide."

MOTIONS:

1. With fingertips together, make a roof of a cabin.
2. Shade eyes with hand as if looking out window.
3. Make a "V" with two fingers and then make hand hop along like the rabbit.
4. Hug self and shiver.
5. Throw hands in air with each "Help!"
6. Make shooting pistols with forefingers.
7. Draw hand towards self, beckoning rabbit.
8. Stroke arm gently from wrist to shoulder with opposite hand, then sniff in sympathy.

Teach song with actions, then eliminate a line of singing each time through until the whole song is done with actions only, no singing.

She'll Be Comin' Round the Mountain

Traditional

A
She'll be com - in' round the moun-tain when she
comes, TOOT! TOOT! She'll be com - in round the
E
moun - tain when she comes TOOT! TOOT! She'll be
A
com - in round the moun - tain, She'll be
D
E
com - in round the moun - tain, She'll be com - in
A
round the moun-tain when she comes. TOOT! TOOT!

2. She'll be drivin' six white horses when she comes.
   Whoa back! (pull on reins)

3. Oh, we'll all go out to greet her when she comes.
   Hi, babe ! (wave)

4. Then we'll kill the old red rooster when she comes.
   Hack, hack! (make chopping motions)

5. And we'll all have chicken and dumplings when she comes.
   Yum, yum! (rub stomach)

6. Oh, she'll wear her red pajamas when she comes.
   Scratch, scratch! (scratch sides)

7. Oh, she'll have to sleep with Grandma when she comes.
   Snore, Snore! (make snoring sound)

Ah-La-La

David Graham

G
D
C
G
Ah-la - la - la - la - la - la - la - le - lu - ia.
C
G
D
Ah - la - la - la - la - la - la - le - lu - ia.
G
D
C
G
Ah - la - la - la - la - la - la - la - le - lu - ia.
C
G
D7
Ah - la - la - la - la - la - la - la
G
C
G
C
le - lu - ia.

2. Shake a neighbor's hand,
3. Tweek a friends's cheek,
4. Rub another back,
5. Clap another back,
6. Jesus is a friend, He's a friend unto you.

Make up your own verses.

Goose Round

D
1
2
Why shouldn't my goose Sing as well as thy goose,
3
4
When I paid for my goose Twice as much as thine?

Head, Shoulders, Knees & Toes

Tune: Tavern in the Town

C
G7
Head, shoul-ders, knees and toes, Head, shoul-ders, knees and toes.
C7
Dm
D
G7
C
Eyes and ears and mouth—and—nose, Head and shoul-ders, knees and toes.

Motions:
Touch the part of your body that you are singing about.

My Bonnie Lies Over the Ocean

Traditional

A
D
A
My Bon-nie lies o - ver the o - cean, My
B
E7
A
Bon - nie lies o - ver the sea. My Bon-nie lies
D
A
B7
E7
o - ver the o - cean, Oh, bring back my Bon-nie to
A
Chorus: A
D
1
B
E7
me. Bring back, bring back, Bring back my
A
2
B
E7
A
Bon-nie to me, to me. back, Oh, bring back my Bon-nie to me.

MOTIONS:

My-point to self.
Bonnie-outline woman's shape with hands.
Lies-lay head on hands as if sleeping.
Over-make arching motions with hands.
Ocean (Sea)-make wave motions with hands.

Oh-make OK sign with thumb and forefinger.
Bring-make beckoning motion with hands.
Back-reach over shoulders and touch back.
My-point to self.
Bonnie-as before.
To-hold up two fingers.
Me-point to self.

Lu-la-le

A Swaying Song

Traditional

F L R Gm L R L
Lu - la-le, lu - la-le, lu - la - lu-la-le, Lu-la,
C R L F R L R
lu - la, lu - la, lu - la - lu - la-la,
F L R Gm L R
Lu - la - le, lu - la - le, lu - la - lu - la-
L C R L C7 F R-L-R
le, Lu-la, lu - la, lu - la - le.—

DIRECTIONS:

With arms over each other's shoulders, sway left(*L*) or right(*R*) as indicated above music. In groups seated in rows, every other row should start with right instead of left so that the rows are swaying opposite each other.

The Windmill

F
1. If I could have a wind - mill, a
Bb C F
wind-mill a wind - mill, if I could have a
Bb 3 C F
wind-mill; I know what I'd have it do.— I'd

2. I'd have it pump the water, the water, the water,
I'd have it pump the water, up from the river below.

3. And then I'd dig a duck pond....
So the ducks and the geese could swim.

4. The ducks would make their wings flap....
And then they would go quack, quack.

5. The geese would stretch their long necks...
And then they would go, Sss, sss.

MOTIONS:
1. Move outstretched arms back and forth.
2. Pump in rhythm as though using bicycle pump.
3. Motions of digging and throwing dirt, in rhythm.
4. Flap arms at sides like wings.
5. Stretch neck around and hiss at end.

Calliope Song

O - ha - ha, Twee-dle-dee-dee, Um-sis-sis.

INSTRUCTIONS

Divide into four groups, each of three singing the parts above. Bring these in one at a time. The fourth group (or a soloist) sings a song in 3/4 time such as "Daisy", or "The More We Get Together", or "Clementine".

Hallelu

Traditional

Eb
Ab
Eb
Db
Hal-le-lu, Hal-le-lu, Hal-le-lu, Hal-le-lu-jah,
Ab
Eb
1 Ab
2
Ab
Praise ye the Lord. Lord. Praise ye the
Eb
Ab
Lord —— Praise ye the Lord ——
Ha-le-lu-jah
Ha-le-lu-jah
Eb
Ab
Eb7
Ab
Praise ye the Lord —— Praise ye the Lord.
Ha-le-lu-jah

DIRECTIONS:
This song is traditionally divided into two groups. One group sings "Hallelujah" and the other sings "Praise ye the Lord". This is most entertaining when each group stands up while they sing and then sits back down when not singing. (Older folks may just raise their hands.) For even more fun, divide into three groups with the third group singing just the "jah" of the "Hallelujah". In a mixed age group this third group could be all the children.

Call of the Fire

Old Camp Song

The call of the fire
Comes to us through the shadows
That follow the close of the day.

Its flames bring us peace
And the calmness of spirit
That drives all our troubles away.

We are thankful for days
And the joys that they bring us,
For nights and the rest that they bring.

May we go on believing
In this joy we're receiving
Just now round the fire as we sing.

Where Is Thumbkin?

TUNE: Frère Jacques

Traditional

F C F C F

1. Where is thumb - kin? Where is thumb - kin?

C F C F C F

Here I am, here I am. How are you this mor-ning?

C F C F C F

Ver-y well I thank you. Run a - way, run a - way.

2. Where is pointer? . . . (index finger)
3. Where is tall man? . . . (middle finger)
4. Where is weak man? . . . (ring finger)
5. Where is the baby? . . . (pinky)
6. Where is the family? . . . (all five)

Song begins with both hands behind your back. When you sing:

"Here I am,"	Hold up the corresponding finger on one hand (i.e. verse 1: hold up thumb, etc.)
"Here I am."	Hold up corresponding finger on the other hand.
"How are you this morning?"	Wiggle the finger on one hand.
"Very well I thank you."	Wiggle the finger on the other hand, as if answering.
"Run away,"	Quickly put one hand behind your back.
"Run away."	Same with other hand.

White Sand and Gray Sand

3-Part Round

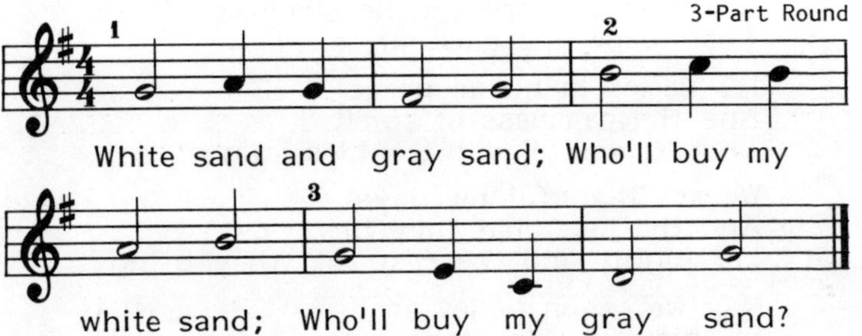
1
2
White sand and gray sand; Who'll buy my
3
white sand; Who'll buy my gray sand?

It's Love

Eb
1. It's love, it's love, it's love that makes the
Bb
makes the world go 'round. It's love, it's
Eb
love that makes the world go 'round. It's love, it's
Bb
love, it's love that makes the world go 'round. It's
Bb7
Eb
love that makes the world go 'round.

2. (Pointing to people all around)
It's you, it's you, it's you that makes the love go 'round.

3. (All stand, move from seats and mingle, shaking hands or hugging.)
So pass it on, God's love is free to everyone.
(Repeat third verse as many times as needed to get people to mix.)

Tommy Tinker

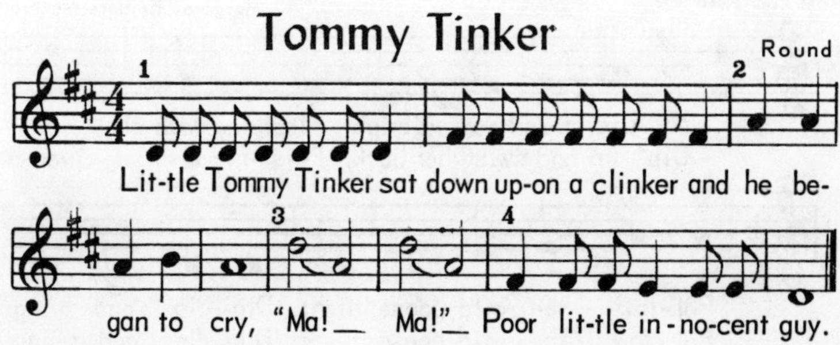
Round
1
2
Lit-tle Tommy Tinker sat down up-on a clinker and he be-
3
4
gan to cry, "Ma!__ Ma!"_ Poor lit-tle in-no-cent guy.

I Love You With the Love of the Lord

J.M.G.
James M. Gilbert
F Gm7
I love you with the love — of the Lord
Am7 Gm7 C7 Fmaj7 F#°
— Yes, I love you with the love —
Gm7 C7 Gm7
of the Lord. — I can see in
C7 A7 Dm
you the glo - ry of my King, and I
Gm7 C7 F
love you with the love — of the Lord. —

As they sing, the people mingle; greeting, shaking hands, perhaps hugging. Sing sing several times.

Canoe Round

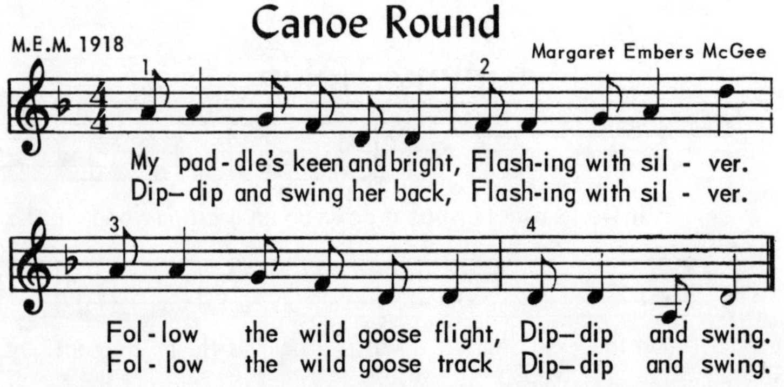
M.E.M. 1918
Margaret Embers McGee
1 2
My pad-dle's keen and bright, Flash-ing with sil - ver.
Dip—dip and swing her back, Flash-ing with sil - ver.
3 4
Fol-low the wild goose flight, Dip—dip and swing.
Fol-low the wild goose track Dip-dip and swing.

Jesus Loves the Little Children

George F. Root

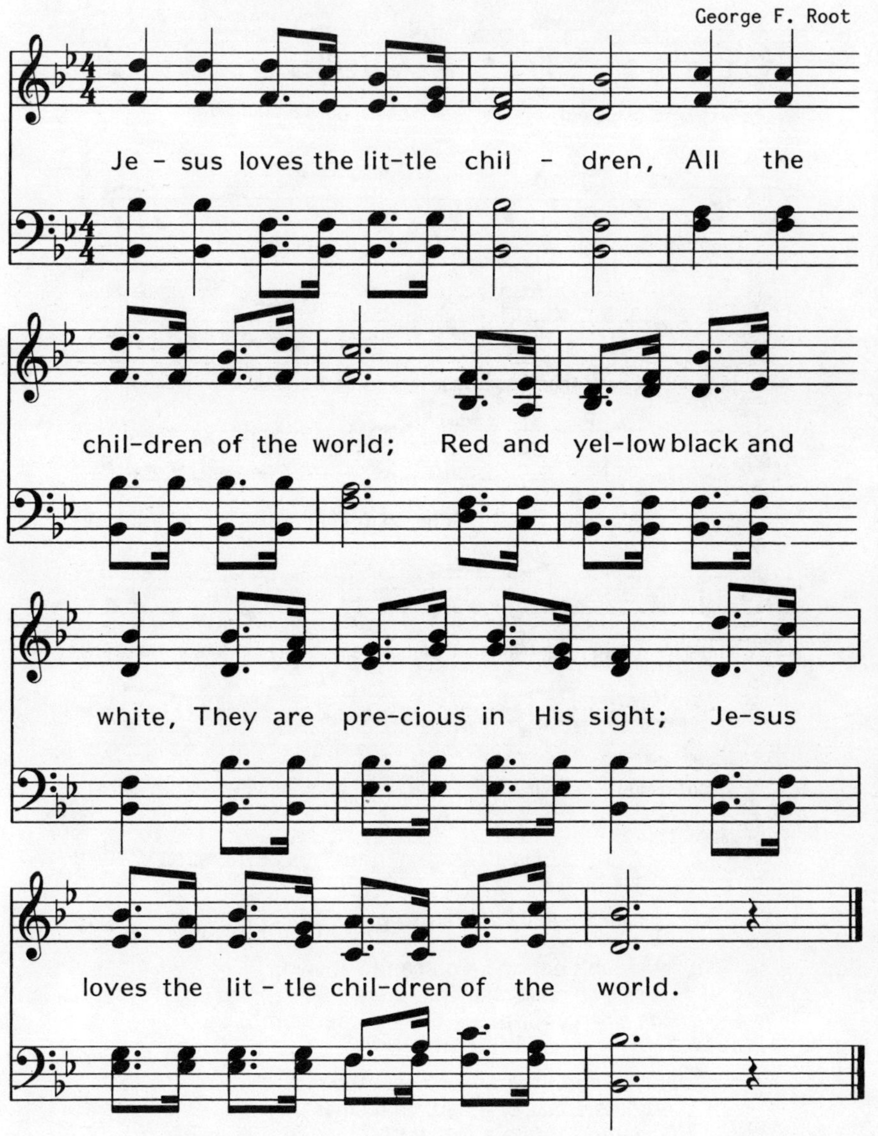
Je - sus loves the lit-tle chil - dren, All the
chil-dren of the world; Red and yel-low black and
white, They are pre-cious in His sight; Je-sus
loves the lit - tle chil-dren of the world.

Chocolate Chip Cookies

Words and music by Bill Steele
Verse
F C
They're made out of sug - ar and but-ter and flour; You
G7 C
put 'em in the ov - en a - bout a quar-ter hour, But the
F C G
thing that gives them their mag-ic power is the choco-late
C Chorus: F C
chips in - side. Choco-late chip cook-ies, I got - ta have
G7 C
more, You can bake 'em in the ov - en, or buy 'em at the store,
F C
But what - ev - er you do, have 'em read - y
G7 C
at the door, And I'll love you till I die.

2. You can't eat one, you can't eat two;
Once you start chewing, there's nothing to do
But clean your plate, and eat the crumbs too,
Then go and find some more.

3. Now when I die, I don't want wings,
A golden halo or a harp that sings.
Give me a book, a fire, and someone that brings me
Chocolate cookies all day.

Peanut Butter and Jelly

F
B♭
F
1. Pea - nut, pea - nut but - ter and jel -

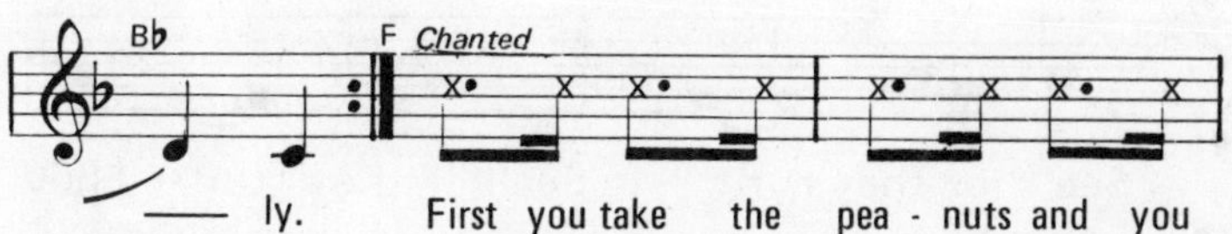
B♭
F Chanted
—— ly. First you take the pea - nuts and you

Dig 'em, you dig 'em, you dig 'em,
smash 'em, you smash 'em, you smash 'em,
spread 'em, you spread 'em, you spread 'em,
1.2.
3.
D.C.
dig 'em, dig 'em, then you 2. Oh,
smash 'em, smash 'em, then you
spread 'em, spread 'em.

2. Oh peanut, peanut butter and jelly.(2x)
   Then you take the berries,
   And you pick'em, you pick'em,
   You pick'em, pick'em, pick'em.
   Then you smash'em, you smash'em,
   You smash'em, smash'em, smash'em.
   Then you spread'em, you spread'em,
   You spread'em, spread'em, spread'em.

3. Oh, peanut, peanut butter and jelly.(2x)
   Then you make the sandwich,
   And you bite it, you bite it,
   You bite it, bite it, bite it.
   Then you chew it, you chew it,
   You chew it, chew it, chew it.
   (slowly) Then you swallow it, you swallow,
   You swallow, swallow, swallow it.

4. Mmm, mm, mm, mm...
   (With mouth closed, do a chewing motion,
   and hum the melody, as if eating and enjoying the sandwich.)

Three Blind Mice
3-part Round
1
Three blind mice! — Three blind mice! —
2
See how they run! — See how they run! – They
3
all ran af-ter the farm - er's wife, She
cut off their tales with a carv - ing knife; Did
you ev - er see such a sight in your
life as three blind mice? —
Chew Your Food
3-part Round
tune: Row Your Boat
1
Chew, chew chew your food, Gent - ly
2
thru the meal, The more you chew, the
3
less you eat, The bet - ter you will feel.

Place in the Choir

Words and Music by Bill Staines

Chorus
G D G D
All God's crit-ters got a place in the choir. Some sing low,
G C G
Some sing high-er, Some sing out loud on the tel-e-phone wire,
Fine
D G
And some just clap their hands, or paws, or an-y-thing they got now.
fins, or claws, or

G D
1. Lis-ten to the bass, it's the one on the bot-tom, Where the bull-frog

G C
croaks and the hip - po - pot - a - mus moans and groans with a

G D G D.C.
big— t'- do.— And the old cow just goes 'moo.'

2. Dogs and the cats they take up the middle,
Where the honey bee hums and the crickets fiddle
The donkey brays and the pony neighs
The old coyote howls (ooww!)

3. Listen to the top where the little birds sing
On the melody with their high notes ringin'
The hoot owl hollers over everything
The jaybird disagrees.

4. Singin' in the night time, singin' in the day
The little duck quacks and is on his way
The possum ain't got much to say
The porcupine talks to himself.

5. It's a simple song of living sung everywhere
By the ox and the fox and the grizzly bear,
The grumpy alligator and the hawk above
The sly raccoon and the turtle dove.

Old MacDonald

Traditional

Old Mac-don-ald had a farm, Ee - i - ee - i
o, And on that farm he had some chicks, Ee-i
ee - i - o. With a chick, chick here, and a
repeat as needed
chick, chick there. Here a chick, there a chick,
ev-'ry-where a chick, chick. Old Mac - don - ald
had a farm, Ee - i - ee - i - o.

2. ducks-quack, quack
3. turkeys-gobble, gobble
4. pigs-oink, oink
5. a Ford-rattle, rattle

Think up other animals and noises.
Each time the song is sung all of the previous animals and noises are repeated in reverse order.

Are You Sleeping?

F
1
2
3
4
Round
Are you sleeping? Brother John, Morning bells are ringing, Ding, ding, dong!

Puffer Billies

4-Part Round
1 F
C7
F
2 F
Down at the sta-tion ear-ly in the morn-ing, See the lit-tle
C7
F
3 F
puf-fer bil-lies all in a row. See the en-gine dri-ver
C7
F
4 F
C7
F
turn a lit-tle han-dle, CHUG, CHUG, PUFF, PUFF, off they go.

2. Down by the seashore, early in the morning,
See the little steamboats all in a row,
See the little sailor turn the little handle:
"Whoop, whoop, whoop, whoop"-Off they go!

3. Down by the seashore, early in the morning,
See the little submarines all in a row,
See the little sailor close the little hatchy,
(make the sound of gurgling water)-Off they go!

4. Down in the kitchen, early in the morning,
See the little doughnuts lying in a row,
Hear the percolator perkin' up the coffee,
"Dunk, dunk, slurp, slurp"-Off they go!

5. Down at the ranch house, early in the morning,
See the little horses standing in a row,
See the little cowboys saddle up the horses,
(make whinneying sound)-Off they go!

6. Down at the airport, early in the morning,
See the little airplanes all in a row,
See the little pilots turn the little handles,
(make airplane noises)-Off they go!

Make New Friends

Moderately slow
Round
1
2
3
4
Make new friends but keep the old; One is sil-ver and the oth-er gold.

Guitar: Eb, Bb each measure

If I Were a Butterfly

Brian Howard

C
F
1. If I were a but-ter - fly I'd thank You, Lord that I had wings
C
G7
and if I were a rob-in in the tree I'd thank You, Lord that
C
I could sing and if I were a fish-y in the sea I'd
F
G7
wig-gle with joy and I'd gig - gle with glee but I just thank You,
C
CHORUS
C
3
Fa - ther for ma - king me me. For you gave me a
3
F
3
heart and you gave me a smile. You gave me Lord Je-sus and you
3
G
C
made me your child but I just thank You, Fa-ther for making me me.

2. If I were an elephant,
I'd thank You, Lord, by raising my trunk.
And if I were a kangaroo,
I'd just hop right up to You.
And if I were an octopus,
I'd thank You, Lord, for my good looks.
But I just thank You, Father, for making me me.

3. If I were a wiggly worm,
I'd thank You, Lord , that I could squirm.
And if I were a crocodile,
I'd thank You, Lord, for my big smile.
And if I were a fuzzy, wuzzy bear,
I'd thank You, Lord, for my fuzzy, wuzzy hair.
But I just thank You, Father for making me me.

If You're Happy

Traditional

F
1. If you're hap - py and you know it, clap your
C
hands. (clap, clap) If you're hap - py and you know it,
F
clap your hands. (clap,clap) If you're hap - py and you
B♭
know it then your face will sure -ly show it, if you're
F
C
hap - py and you know it, clap your hands. (clap, clap)

2. Stamp your feet (stamp, stamp)

3. Nod your head (nod, nod)

4. Do all three (all together)

Beans In Your Ears

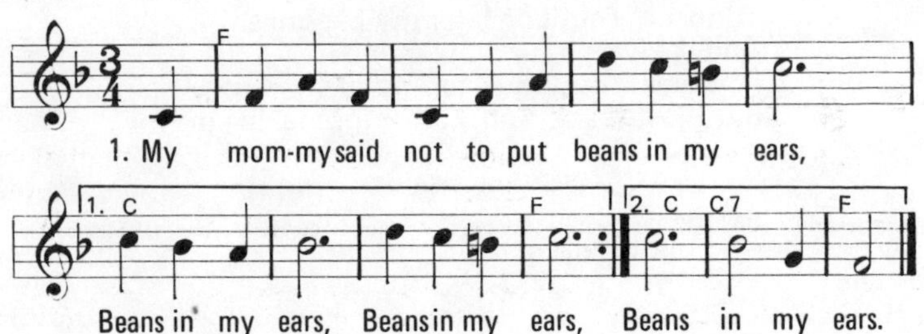
F
1. My mom-my said not to put beans in my ears,
1. C
F
2. C C7
F
Beans in my ears, Beans in my ears, Beans in my ears.

2. Now why would I want to put beans in my ears?
3. You can't hear your leader with beans in your ears.
4. Then, maybe I ought to put beans in my ears.
5. Hey, *(Somebody's name)* , Let's go and put beans in our ears.
6. (That person's answer:) You'll have to speak up, I've got beans in my ears.
7. I think that all grown-ups have beans in their ears.

Note: Editor not responsible if children put beans in their ears.

We're Sorry You're Going Away

Tune: Blest Be the Tie

F C F
We're sor - ry you're go - ing a - way,
Bb F C
We wish— that you— could stay!
C F C7
We know we will miss you, We wish we could
F Bb F C7 F C7 F
kiss you, We're sor - ry you're go - ing a - way.

Jesus Loves Me

Anna B. Warner — William B. Bradbury

1. Je-sus loves me! this I know, For the Bi-ble tells me so;
2. Je-sus loves me! He who died Heav-en's gate to o-pen wide;
3. Je-sus take this heart of mine, Make it pure and whol-ly Thine;
Lit-tle ones to Him be-long, They are weak but He is strong.
He will wash a-way my sin, Let His lit-tle child come in.
On the cross You died for me, I will try to live for Thee.
Yes, Je - sus loves me! Yes, Je - sus loves me!
Yes, Je - sus loves me! The Bi-ble tells me so.

Turn It Over to Jesus

Turn it o - ver to Je-sus,— Turn it o-ver to
Je-sus,— Turn it o-ver to Je-sus — ev'-ry
thing's gon-na be all right! all —— right ——
all —— right —— all ——
right,— ev'-ry thing's gon-na be all right!

Adapted from a song by Ray Hildebrand.

Thank You for the World So Sweet

E. Rutter Leatham
Thank you for the world so sweet; Thank you
for the food we eat; Thank you for the birds that
sing; Thank you, God, for ev-'ry-thing. A-men.

Follow the Gleam

Helen Hill Miller — Sallie Hume Douglas

G C G
1. To the knights in the days of old
Came a vi-sion of Ho - ly Grail
D7 1G
Keep-ing watch on the moun-tain height,
And a voice through the wait-ing
2G D G7 C G
night. Fol - low fol - low, fol - low the
D7 G
gleam, Ban-ner's un-furled o'er all the
D G7 C G
world, Fol - low, fol - low, fol - low the
D7 G
gleam of the Chal-ice that is the Grail.

2. And we who would serve the King
And loyally Him obey,
In the consecrate silence know
That the challenge still holds today.

Follow, follow, follow the gleam,
Standards of worth o'er all the earth.
Follow, follow, follow the gleam
Of the light that shall bring the dawn.

Note: Especially for dedication or commitment for youth, using candles.

I Love Him Better Every Day

S.E.C. | Sidney E. Cox

I love Him bet-ter ev-'ry day, —— I love Him
ev-'ry day,
bet-ter ev-'ry day; —— Close by His side
ev-'ry day;
poco rit.
I will a-bide — I love Him bet-ter ev-'ry day.

Alternate version:

I love Him better ev'ry d-a-y,
I love Him better ev'ry d-a-y;
Close by His s-i-d-e I will a-b-i-d-e,
I love Him better ev'ry d-a-y.

Peace Like a River

F F7

I've got peace like a riv-er I've got

B♭ F

peace like a riv - er, I've got peace like a

Dm G7 Gm7/C C7 F

riv-er in my soul, —— I've got peace like a

F7 B♭ F

riv-er, I've got peace like a riv-er, I've got

Dm F/C C7 F

peace like a riv-er in — my soul! ——

2. I've got pain like an arrow...
3. I've got strength like a mountain...
4. I've got joy like a fountain...
5. I've got fear like an iceberg...
6. I've got love like the sunshine...
7. I've got de-ter-mi-na-tion...

Row Your Boat

D 1
2
Round
Row, row, row your boat Gen - tly down the stream;
3
4
Mer-ri-ly, mer-ri-ly, mer-ri-ly, mer-ri-ly, Life is but a dream.

I've Got the Joy

C Em Am C G C
1. I've got the joy, joy, joy, joy down in my heart,
G7 C
*Down in my heart,*down in my heart; I've got the
C Em Am C G C
joy, joy, joy, joy, down in my heart,
G7 C
*Down in my heart to stay.

*"Where?"

2. I've got the peace that passeth understanding,
Down in my heart, etc.

3. I've got the love of Jesus, love of Jesus,
Down in my heart.

Whippoorwill

Anne H. Chapin
3-Part Round

1 F C7 F
Gone to bed is the set - ing sun,
2 F C7 F
Night is com-ing and day is done, Whip-poor-
4 F C7 F
will, whip-poor-will, has just— be-gun.

The Orchestra

Austrian Folk Song

B♭ F7
The vi - o - lins play - ing, are ring - ing —
B♭ F7
and — sing - ing, The vi - o-lins play-ing are
B♭ B♭
like — a — love-ly song. The clar-i-nets, the
F7 1 B♭
clar-i-nets, play du-a, du-a, du-a, du-a det.
2 B♭ B♭ F7 B♭
det. The horns, the horns wake us at morn.
B♭ F7
The trum-pets are blar-ing, ta-ta ta-ta-ta-ta-ta
1 B♭ 2 B♭ B♭
ta-ta-ta-ta ta - ta-ta-ta. The ta. The
F7 B♭
tu-ba plays two notes and al-ways the same notes
F7 B♭
five, one, one, five, five, five, five, five, one.

Down By the Old Millstream

F Db7 C7 F C7
Down by the old mill - stream, Where I first met
F Bb C7
you, With your eyes so blue, Dressed in ging - ham
F Db7 C7 F/C C# dim6
too, It was there I knew, That you loved me
Dm Db
true,— You were six - teen,— My vil - age
F G7 C7 F
queen,— Down by the old mill stream.——

Version 2:

Down by the old (not the new but the old)
  millstream(not the river but the stream),
Where I first (not last but first)
  met you (not me but you),
With your eyes (not ears but eyes)
  so blue (not green but blue),
Dressed in ging— (not calico but ging—)
  ham, too (not three but two),
It was there (not here but there)
  I knew (not old but new),
That you loved (not hated but loved)
  me true (not false but true).
You were sixteen (not fifteen but sixteen),
My village queen (not king but queen),
Down by the old (not the new but the old)
  millstream (not the river but the stream)

The Happy Wanderer

Antonia Ridge
Friedr. W. Möller
I love to go a-wan-der-ing, A-long the
moun-tain track,— And as I go, I love to
sing, My knap-sack on my back.— Val-de
ri — Val-de ra — Val-de ra — Val-de
ha ha ha ha ha ha Val-de ri, — Val-de
ra. — My knap-sack on my back.—

2. I love to wander by the stream
   That dances in the sun,
   So joyously it calls to me,
   "Come! Join my happy song!"

3. I wave my hat to all I meet,
   And they wave back to me,
   And blackbirds call so loud and sweet
   From ev'ry green-wood tree.

4. High overhead, the skylarks wing,
   They never rest at home
   But just like me, they love to sing,
   As o'er the world we roam.

5. Oh, may I go awandering
   Until the day I die!
   Oh, may I always laugh and sing,
   Beneath God's clear blue sky!

Each Campfire Lights Anew

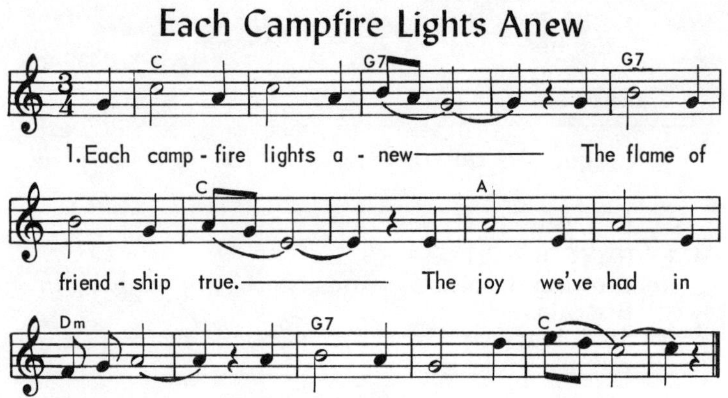
C
G7
G7
1. Each camp - fire lights a - new——— The flame of
C
A
friend - ship true.——— The joy we've had in
Dm
G7
C
know-ing you——— Will last our whole life through.———

2. And as the embers die away,
We wish we could forever stay,
But since we cannot have our way
We'll come again some other day.

Clementine

Traditional

G
1. In a cav-ern, in a can-yon, Ex-ca-
D7
va— ting for a mine, lived a min-er for-ty-
G
D7
G
nin - er, And his daugh-ter Clem-en-tine.

CHORUS:
Oh, my darling, oh, my darling
Oh, my darling Clementine.
You are lost and gone forever,
Dreadful sorry, Clementine.

2. Light she was and like a fairy,
And her shoes were number nine.
Herring boxes without topses,
Sandals were for Clementine.

3. Drove she ducklings to the water,
Every morning just at nine.
Hit her toe against a splinter,
Fell into the foaming brine.

4. Ruby lips above the water,
Blowing bubbles soft and fine.
But alas!, I was no swimmer,
So I lost my Clementine.

5. Now you all should learn the moral
Of this little tale of mine;
Artificial respiration
Would have saved my Clementine.

I Love the Mountains

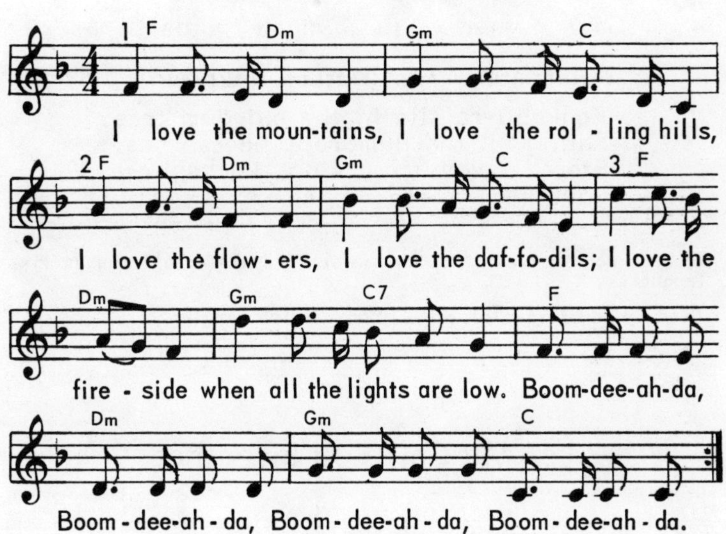
1 F
Dm
Gm
C
I love the moun-tains, I love the rol - ling hills,
2 F
Dm
Gm
C
3 F
I love the flow - ers, I love the daf-fo-dils; I love the
Dm
Gm
C7
F
fire - side when all the lights are low. Boom-dee-ah-da,
Dm
Gm
C
Boom - dee-ah - da, Boom - dee-ah - da, Boom - dee-ah - da.

Repeat *ad lib* or use as a round.

French Cathedrals

E
1
2
3
Or-lé-ans,Beau-gen-cy,No-tre Dame de Clé-ry,Ven-dô-me,Ven-dô-me.

Kookaburra

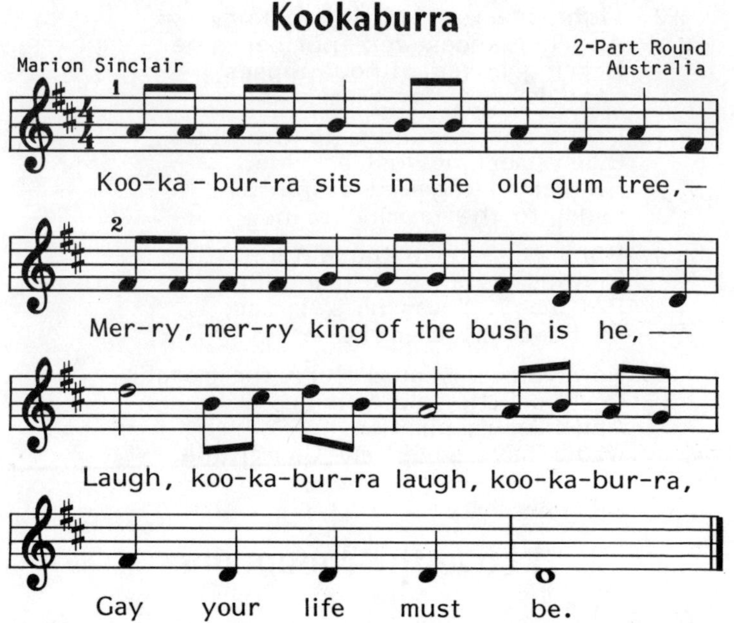
2-Part Round
Marion Sinclair
Australia
1
Koo-ka - bur-ra sits in the old gum tree,—
2
Mer-ry, mer-ry king of the bush is he,—
Laugh, koo-ka-bur-ra laugh, koo-ka-bur-ra,
Gay your life must be.

Alternate words (author unknown):

Kookaburra sits in the old gum tree,
Eating all the gumdrops he can see.
Stop, kookaburra, stop, kookaburra,
Save some there for me.

Kookaburra is a large Australian seabird whose call sounds like laughter.

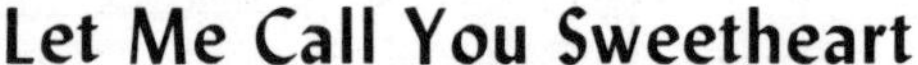

Let Me Call You Sweetheart

Beth Slater Whitson
Leo Friedman
B♭ F7 B♭ C♯dim B♭
Let me call you sweet - heart, I'm in
E♭ G7/D C7 F F7
love with you.— Let me hear you

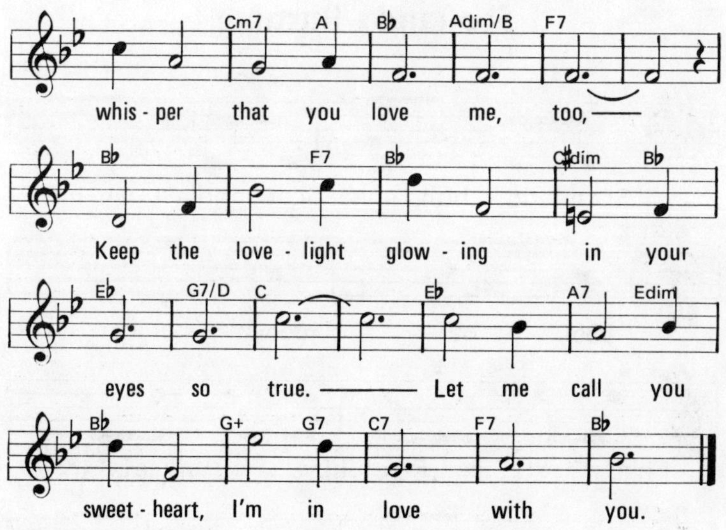
Cm7 A B♭ Adim/B F7
whis - per that you love me, too,
B♭ F7 B♭ C♯dim B♭
Keep the love - light glow - ing in your
E♭ G7/D C E♭ A7 Edim
eyes so true. Let me call you
B♭ G+ G7 C7 F7 B♭
sweet - heart, I'm in love with you.

Sing again omitting all pronouns: (Me, I'm, you, your)

Courtesy of Shawnee Press, Inc.; Delaware Water Gap, PA 18327

Ahrirang

Korean Folk Song

G G G D7
Ah - ri - rang, Ah - ri - rang, Ah - ri - ri - o,
Em C G G C G
As you pro - ceed a - long Ah - ri - ran pass,
Bm Bm Em C D7
1. You, my loved one, who me have for - sa - ken,
2. Blue the sky with its my - ri - ad stars, so
Em C G G C
Pain - ed be your feet at the end of a mile.
Sad-ness fills my heart with its my - ri - ad woes.

Courtesy Lynn Gault and Bliss Wiant

Scotland's Burning

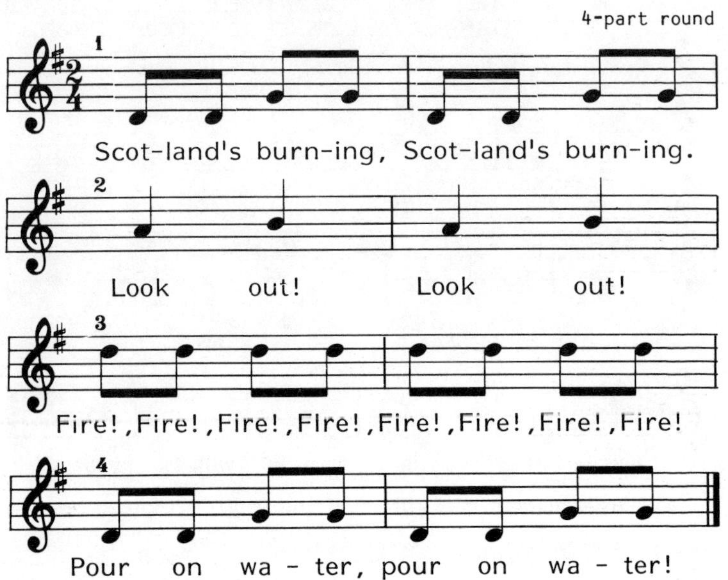
4-part round
1
Scot-land's burn-ing, Scot-land's burn-ing.
2
Look out! Look out!
3
Fire!,Fire!,Fire!,Fire!,Fire!,Fire!,Fire!,Fire!
4
Pour on wa - ter, pour on wa - ter!

Old Smoky

Moderately fast, lightly
C F C
1. On top of old Smo - ky, all cov-ered with snow,—
G C
I — lost my true lov - er by court-ing too slow.—

2. A-courting is pleasure and a-parting is grief,
But a false-hearted lover is worse than a thief.

3. A thief will but rob you of all that you save,
But a false-hearted lover will send you to the grave.

4. Your grave will decay you and turn you to dust.
Not a boy in ten thousand a poor girl can trust.

5. I'll go to Old Smoky, the mountains so high,
Where the wild birds and turtle doves can hear my sad cry.

Tell Me Why

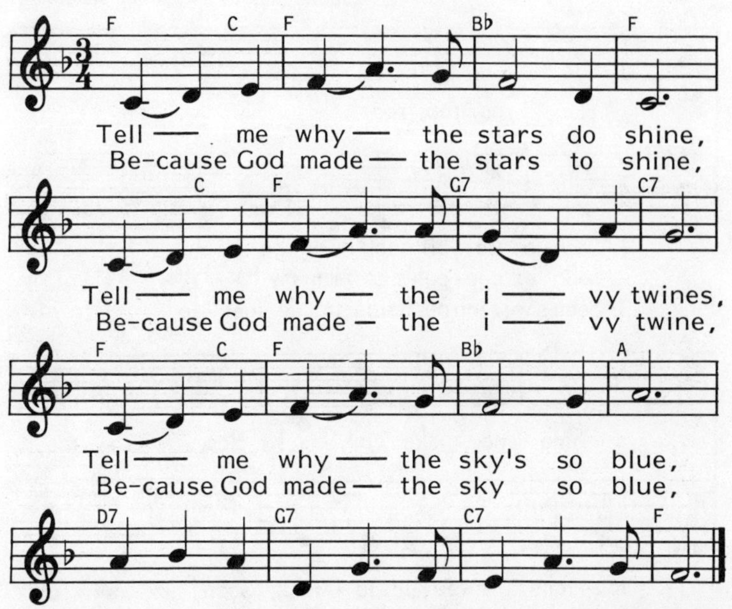
Tell — me why — the stars do shine,
Be-cause God made — the stars to shine,
Tell — me why — the i — vy twines,
Be-cause God made — the i — vy twine,
Tell — me why — the sky's so blue,
Be-cause God made — the sky so blue,
And I will tell you just why I love you.
Be-cause God made you, that's why I love you.

Morning Comes Early

Katherine Davis
Slovakian Folk Song
Morn-ing comes ear-ly and bright with dew, Un-der your win-dow I sing to you. Up, then, my com-rade, up, then, my com-rade, Let us be greet-ing the morn so blue.
Why do you lin-ger so long in bed? O-pen your win-dow and show your head. Up, then, with singing, up, then, with sing-ing, O-ver the mead-ows the sun comes red.

From "Ten Folk Songs and Ballads," © 1931, E.C. Schirmer. By permission

* Other voices may enter for a 2-part round.

Sweet Potatoes

English by H.W.L.

Creole Folk Song
Counter Melody by Hector Spaulding

Roo, roo, roo, roo, hoo, hoo,
1. Soon ez we - all cook swee' pe-ta-tehs, swee' pe-
2. Soon ez sup - peh's et, Mam-my hol - lehs, Mam - my
3. Soon's we tech our haids to de peel - lo, to de
Sing ho - ke-dink - um! Roo, roo, roo,
ta - tehs, swee' pe - ta - tehs, Soon ez we - all
hol - lehs, Mam - my hol - lehs, Soon ez sup - peh's
peel - lo, to de peel - lo, Soon's we tech our
roo, hoo, hoo, hoo, hoo!
cook swee' pe - ta - tehs, Eat 'em right straight up!
et, Mam - my hol - lehs, "Git a - long to baid!"
haids to de peel - lo, Go to sleep right smart!

Rose, Rose

Round

1 Rose, rose, 2 rose, rose, Shall I ev-er see thee red?
3 Aye, mar-ry, that thou wilt, 4 If thou but stay.

Home on the Range

Brewster Higley (1873) Cowboy U. S. A.

1. Oh, — give me a home where the buf-fa-lo roam, Where the deer and the an - te-lope play, — Where sel-dom is heard a dis-cour-ag-ing word, And the skies are not cloud-y all day. —

2. Where the air is so pure and the zeph-yrs so free, And the bree-zes so balm-y and light, — That I would not ex-change my home on the range, For — all of the cit-ies so bright. —

Chorus

Home, home on the range, — Where the deer and the an - te-lope play, — Where sel-dom is heard a dis-cour-ag-ing word, And the skies are not cloud-y all day. —

Back of the Bread

C
F
Back of the bread is the flour and back of the
C
G
flour is the mill and back of the mill is the
F
C
G7
C
sun and the rain and the Fa - ther's will.

Cielito Lindo

Mexico

Bb F7 Bb F7
1. From Si - er— ra Mo - re-na, Cie— li - to
1. De la Sie— ra Mo - re-na, Cie— li - to
Bb Dm Cm
Lin-do comes— soft-ly steal-ing,—
Lin-do vie— ne ba - jan-do,—
F7
Laugh-ing eyes— black and rogu-ish, Cie-
Un par de‿o— ji - tos ne-gros, Cie-
Bb
— li - to Lin-do, beau— ty re-veal-ing.—
— li - to Lin-do, de—con-tra-ban-do.—
CHORUS Eb G7 C7 F7 Bb
Ay, ay, ay, ay!— Sing, ban-ish sor-row.
¡Ay, ay, ay, ay!— Can - ta‿y no llo-res.
— To pass the hours— light-ly
— Por - que can-tan— do se‿a-
F7
sing - ing, Cie— li - to Lin - do glad-
le - gran, Cie— li - to Lin - do, los-
Bb
— dens the mor - row.—
— co - ra - zo - nes.—

2. In the air brightly flashing, Cielito Lindo, flies Cupid's feather.
In my heart it is striking, Cielito Lindo, wounding forever.

2. *Una flecha en el aire, Cielito Lindo, lanzó Cupido,*
Y como fué jugando, Cielito Lindo, yo fuí el herido.

Over the Meadows

Eng. by A.D.Z.
In hiking time
Czech
G C G G D7 G G C G C Am D7 G
O-ver the mead-ows green and wide, Bloom-ing in the
Sweet is the air with new-mown hay, Cool-ing in the
sun-light, Bloom-ing in the sun-light, O-ver the meadows
twi-light, Cool-ing in the twi-light, Sweet is the air with
green and wide, Off we go a-roam-ing side by side.
new-mown hay, As we homeward go at close of day.
HEY!
CHORUS
G C D7 G D7
Stream-lets down mountain go, Pure from the winter snow,
Join-ing, they swift-ly go, Sing-ing of life so free.
G C D7 G
Stream-lets down mountain go, Pure from the winter snow,
Join-ing, they swift-ly go, Call-ing to me!

Waltzing Matilda

Australia
A.B. Patterson
Marie Cowan
Eb Bb7 Eb
1. Once a jol - ly swag-man camped by a
Ab Eb
bil - a-bong, un - der the shade of a
Bb Eb Bb7
coo-li-bah tree, And he sang as he sat and
Eb Ab Eb
wait-ed while his bil - ly boiled: "You'll come a-
Bb7 Eb Fine
waltz - ing Ma - til - da with me."
Eb Ab
"Waltz-ing Ma-til - da, waltz-ing Ma-til - da,
Eb Ab Eb Bb7 Bb D.S.
You'll come a-waltz-ing Ma - til - da with me."

2. Down came a jumbuck, to drink at the billabong,
Up jumped the swagman; grabbed him with glee,
And he sang as he shoved that jumbuck in his
tuckerbag:
"You'll come a-waltzing Matilda with me."

3. Down came the squatter mounted on his thorobred,
Up came the troopers, one, two, three,
"Who's that jolly jumbuck you've got in your
tuckerbag?
You'll come a-waltzing Matilda with me."

4. Up jumped the swagman sprang into the billabong,
"You'll never catch me alive!" said he.
And his ghost may be heard as you pass by
that billabong:
"You'll come a-waltzing Matilda with me."

Expanations: Swagman-tramp; Billabong-waterhole; Coolibah-eucalyptus; Billy-tin can used as kettle; Waltzing Matilda-tramping with a bundle(swag); Jumbuck-sheep; Tucker-food; Squatter-rancher; Trooper-sherrif.

The Upward Trail

Traditional
G
We're on the up-ward trail! We're on the
C
D7
up-ward trail! Singing, singing, ev'-ry-bod-y
G
singing, As we go! We're on the up-ward
C
D7
trail! We're on the up-ward trail! Singing,
G
singing, ev-ry-bod-y singing, On we go!

Johnny Appleseed's Grace

K.G. & W.K
Kim Gannon & Walter Kent
F
Oh, the Lord is good to me, And
C7
F
so I thank the Lord, For giv-ing me the
Am
C7
things I need, The sun and the rain and the
F
C7
F
ap-ple seed; The Lord is good to me.

2. And every seed that grows
Will grow into a tree.
And one day soon there'll be apples there,
For everyone in the world to share.
The Lord is good to me.

Second verse by kind permission of the Girl Guide Association (UK). From the Diamond Jubilee Song Book.

Praise for Bread

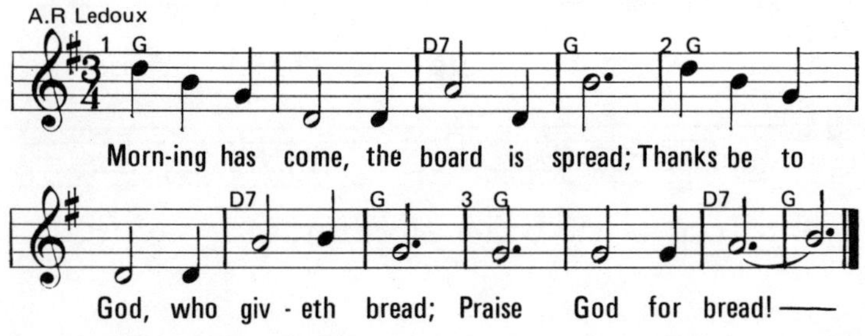
A.R Ledoux
1 G
D7
G
2 G
Morn-ing has come, the board is spread; Thanks be to
D7
G
3 G
D7
G
God, who giv - eth bread; Praise God for bread! ——

Also sing "Noontime" and "Evening".

Cuckoo

English by Katherine F. Rohrbough

Austria

F
C7
Oh, I went to Pe-ter's flow-ing spring
G
C7
F
where the wa-ter's so good; And I heard there
C7
G
C7
F
the cuc— koo as she called from the wood.
A
F
G
C7
F
1
2
3
Ho - li - ah, Ho - le-rah - hi - hi - ah,
C7
1
2
B
1
2
3
Ho- le - rah cuc-koo, Ho - le-rah - hi - hi - ah,
F
1
2
B
1
2
3
Ho - le-rah cuc-koo, Ho - li - rah - hi - hi - ah,
C7
1
2
B
1
2
3
F
1
Ho-le-rah cuc-koo, Ho-le-ra - hi-hi-ah - ho.

INSTRUCTIONS:

A-Patter on knees.

1-Slap knees; 2-Clap hands; 3-Snap fingers.

B-Snap fingers and sing "cuckoo"; onces the first time through, twice the second time and so on, adding another snap and "cuckoo" each time.

Other verses:

1. After Easter come sunny days that will melt all the snow;
   Then I'll marry my maiden fair, we'll be happy I know.
2. When I've married my maiden fair what then can I desire?
   Oh, a home for our tending and some wood for the fire.

You Are My Sunshine

Jimmie Davis & Charles Mitchell

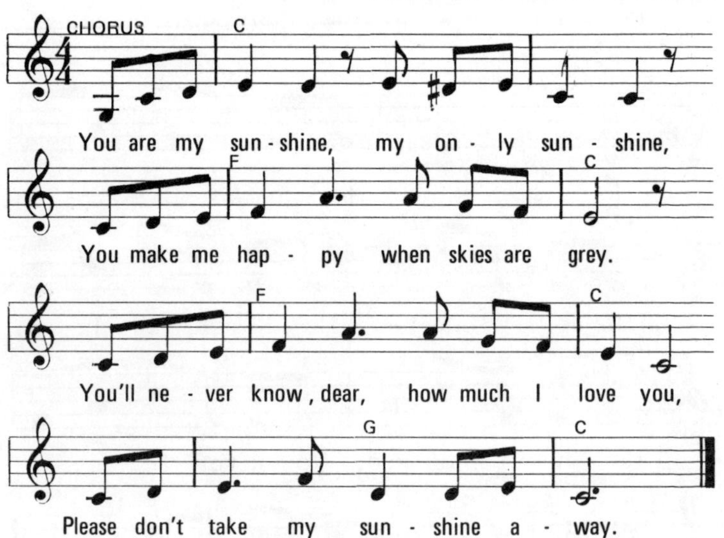
CHORUS
C
You are my sun-shine, my on-ly sun-shine,
F
C
You make me hap-py when skies are grey.
F
C
You'll ne-ver know, dear, how much I love you,
G
C
Please don't take my sun-shine a-way.

1. The other night, dear, as I lay sleeping,
   I dreamed I held you by my side.
   When I awoke, dear, I was mistaken;
   And I hung my head and I cried.
   CHORUS

2. I'll always love you and make you happy,
   If you will only say the same.
   But if you leave me to love another,
   You'll regret it all some day.
   CHORUS

Cindy

American Folk Song

Bb
F
Bb
Eb
Bb
F
Bb
I wish I had a nick-el, I wish I had a dime, I
wish I had a pret-ty lit-tle girl To love me all the time.
Chorus
3
Eb
3
Bb
Get a-long home, Cindy, Cindy, Get a-long home, Cindy, Cindy,
3
Eb
Bb
F7
Bb
Get a-long home, Cindy, Cindy, I'll mar-ry you some-day.

2.

I went to see my Cindy, she met me at the door,
With shoes and stockings in her hand
And her feet all over the floor.

3.

She took me to the parlor, She cooled me with her fan.
She told me I was the prettiest thing
In the shape of mortal man.

4.

Cindy in the spring-time, Cindy in the fall,
If I can't have my Cindy gal,
I'll have no gal at all.

Hey, Ho! Nobody Home

3-Part Round

1
2
Hey, ho! No - bod-y home, Meat nor drink nor
3
mon-ey have I none, Yet will I be mer - - ry!

For He's a Jolly Good Fellow

Traditional

G C G D7
For he's a jol-ly good fel-low, for he's a

G
jol-ly good fel-low, for he's a jol-ly good

C G D7 G
fel-low, which no-bo-dy can de-ny!— Which

C G
no-bo-dy can de-ny!— Which no-bo-dy

C G
can de-ny!— For he's a jo-ly good

C G D7 D
fel— low, Which no-bo-dy can de-ny!

Hark to the Chimes

G D G
Hark to the chimes, Come, bow your head,
D G
We thank Thee, Lord, For this good bread.

Good Night, Ladies

Author unknown
Bb
1. Good-night, la - dies! — Good-night,
F7 Bb Eb
la-dies! — Good-night, la-dies! We're
Bb F7 Bb
going to leave you now. Me-ri-ly we roll a-long,
1 F7 Bb 2 F7 Bb
roll a-long, roll a-long, O'er the dark blue sea.

2. Farewell, ladies, farewell, ladies,
Farewell, ladies, we're going to leave you now.
Merrily we roll along, etc.

3. Sweet dreams, ladies, sweet dreams ladies,
Sweet dreams, ladies, we're going to leave
you now.
Hope you've had a happy time, happy time,
happy time,
Hope you've had a happy time,
We've had a good time, too.

Chinese Grace

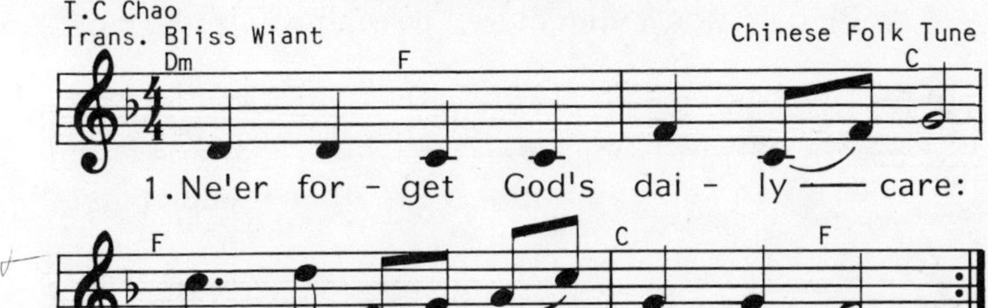
T.C Chao
Trans. Bliss Wiant
Chinese Folk Tune
Dm F C
1.Ne'er for - get God's dai - ly — care:
F C F
Health and food — and — clothes to wear.

2.Freely we these gifts receive.
May we not His Spirit grieve.

Workin' on the Railroad

Traditional American

G
C
I've been work-in' on the rail - road all the
G
live long day — I've been work-in' on the
A7
D
D7
rail-road to pass the time a - way. Can't you
G
C
hear the whist-le blow- in', rise up so ear-ly
B7
C
in the morn; Can't you hear the cap-'n
G
A7
D7
G
shout - in', "Di - nah blow your horn."
C
Di-nah won't you blow, Di-nah won't you blow,
D7
G
D7
G
Di - nah won't you blow your horn, your horn?
C
Di - nah won't you blow, Di-nah won't you blow,

D7
G
Di-nah won't you blow your horn?
G
Some-one's in the kitch-en with Di - nah,
D
Some-one's in the kitch-en I know,
G
C
Some-one's in the kitch-en with Di - nah,
G
D7
G
Strum-min' on the old ban - jo and sing-in'
3
Fee - fi fid-dle-ee - i - o, Fee - fi-
3
D
G
fid-dle-ee - i - o, Fee - fi-
C
3
G
D7
G
fid-dle-ee-i - o, strum-min' on the old ban-jo.

El Shaddai

Michael Card & John Thompson
Unison
Fm Bb
El Shad-dai, El Shad-dai, El El-
Eb Cm Db G
yon na A - do - nai; age to age you're still the same
Cm G/D C/E Fm
by the pow-er of the name. El Shad-dai El Shad-dai,
Bb Eb Cm
er-kahm - ka na A - do-nai; we will
Db Bb Bb7 Eb
praise and lift you high El Shad-dai.

The words of El Shaddai mean:

El Shaddai: God Almighty
na Adanoi: O Lord
El Elyon: The most high God
Erkahmka: We will love you

God and Man at Table

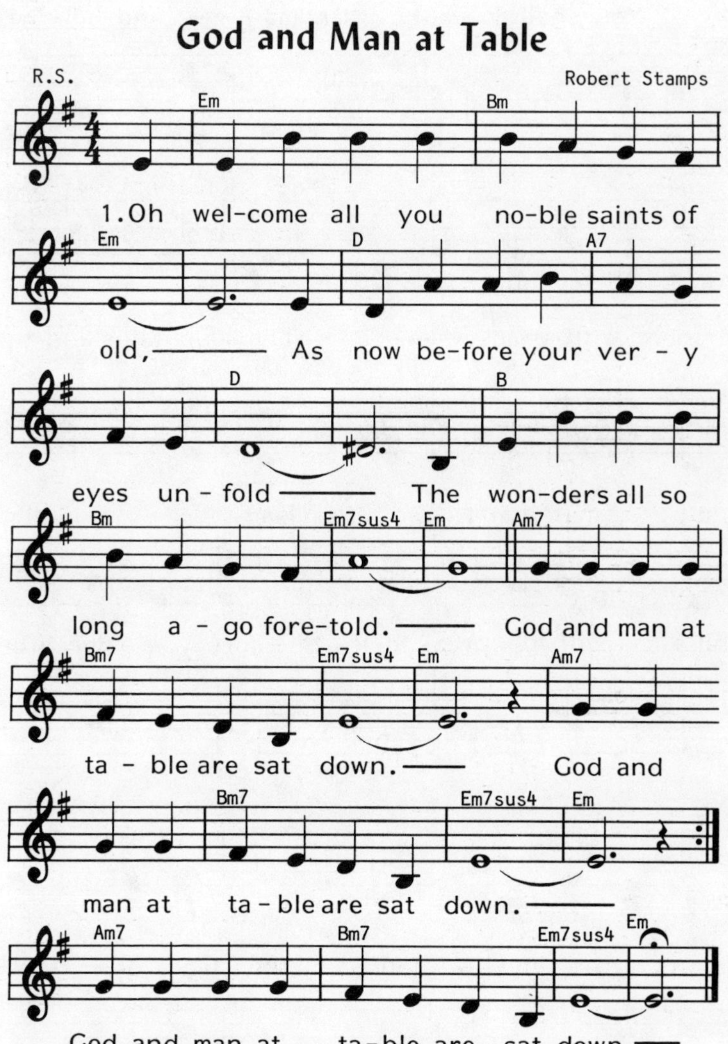
R.S.
Robert Stamps
Em
Bm
1. Oh wel-come all you no-ble saints of
Em
D
A7
old, As now be-fore your ver - y
D
B
eyes un - fold The won-ders all so
Bm
Em7sus4
Em
Am7
long a - go fore-told. God and man at
Bm7
Em7sus4
Em
Am7
ta - ble are sat down. God and
Bm7
Em7sus4
Em
man at ta - ble are sat down.
Am7
Bm7
Em7sus4
Em
God and man at ta-ble are sat down.

Trees of the Field

Isaiah 55;12
adapted S.G. Rubin

Stuart Dauerman

Em
You shall go out with joy — and be led
D7/F#
G
forth with peace. — The moun-tains and the
C/G
G
D/F#
D7
B/D#
hills will break forth be - fore you; There'll be
Em
shouts of joy, — and all the trees of — the

Em/B B7 Em/B B7 Em Fine
field will clap, will clap their hands.
D7 G C/G G
And all the trees of the field will
D
1
clap their hands (clap,clap) The trees of the
G
field will clap their hands (clap,clap) The
2 B7 C6 C#o7 B7/D# Em D.C. al Fine
While you go out with joy

I Live, I Live

R.C. Rich Cook

I live, I live, be-cause He is ris - en. I
live, I live with pow'r o-ver sin. I
to wor—— ship Him. Thank you
Je - sus, thank you Je —— sus. Be-cause you're a-live,
be-cause you're a-live, be-cause you're a-live, I live!——
1
2

I Will Sing

Max Dyer

M.D
D
A/C#
Bm
D/A
1. I will sing, I will sing a song un-to the Lord.

Em
A7
D
G/A
I will sing, I will sing a song un-to the Lord.

D
A/C#
Bm
D/A
I will sing, I will sing a song un-to the Lord.

Em
A7
D G/D D
Al - le - lu - ia, Glo - ry to the Lord.

Chorus:
Allelu, alleluia, glory to the Lord.
Allelu, alleluia, glory to the Lord.
Allelu, alleluia, glory to the Lord.
Alleluia, glory to the Lord.

2. We will come, we will come as one before the Lord. (3x)
Alleluia, glory to the Lord.

3. If the Son, if the Son shall make you free, (3x)
You shall be free indeed.

4. They that sow in tears shall reap in joy. (3x)
Alleluia, glory to the Lord.

5. Ev'ry knee shall bow and ev'ry tongue confess, (3x)
That Jesus Christ is Lord.

6. In His name, in His name we have the victory. (3x)
Alleluia, glory to the Lord.

We Are the Family of God

John Byron

CHORUS
D A Bm G
We are the fam-ily of God, Yes,
D A
We are the fam-ily of God; And He's
D A Bm7
brought us to-geth-er to be one in Him, That
G A D G D Fine
we might bring light to the world.
Dmaj7 D7
1. Go, make dis - ci-ples of all lives;
G G/F# Asus A
Go, show them my way is true.
D F# Bm
Tell them the won-der-ful sto-ry That
E A A7 D.C.
they might be one in me too.

2. Let them know life in the making,
Let them know peace from above,
Show them by your own example
Of love in the family of God.

3. Bigger and better is my love
That I have bestowed unto you;
And now it's for each one to share of
That all things might now become new.

The Joy of the Lord

Alliene G. Vale

E♭
1. The joy of the Lord
B♭7
is my strength. The joy of the
A♭/E♭ E♭
Lord is my strength. The
joy of the Lord
A♭ E♭
is my strength. The joy of the
B♭7 E♭
Lord is my strength.

John 4:14

2. He gives me living water and I thirst no more. (3x)
The joy of the Lord is my strength.

3. He fills my heart with laughter, ha, ha, ha, ha, ha. (3x)
The joy of the Lord is my strength.

I Am the Light of the World

J.S. Jim Strathdee

CHORUS
F G C Am
"I am the light of the world
F G C Am C Am
You peo-ple come and fol-low me!" If you
F G C Am
fol-low and love, you'll learn the mys-ter-y
F G C
of what you were meant to do and be.
VERSE
F G C
1. When the song of the an-gels is stilled, When the
Dm Am G
star in the sky is gone, When the
C F G
kings and the shep-herds have found their way
C Am F G
home, The work of Christ-mas has be-gun!

In response to a Christmas poem by Howard Thurman.

2. To find the lost and lonely one,
To heal that broken soul with love,
To feed the hungry children,
With warmth and good food,
To feel the earth below the sky above!

3. To free the prisoner from his chains,
To make the powerful care,
To rebuild the nations
With strength of goodwill,
To see God's children everywhere!

4. To bring hope to every task you do,
To dance at a baby's new birth,
To make music in an old person's heart,
And sing to the colors of the earth.

Glorify Thy Name

D.A.
Donna Adkins
C F/C G7
1.Fa - ther we love Thee, we praise Thee, we a-
C C/E F G7/F
dore Thee. Glo - ri-fy Thy Name in all the
C/E Dm7 G7 C/E F
earth. Glo - ri - fy Thy Name.
E Am Fm6/Ab C/G Em7 Eb°7
Glo - ri - fy Thy Name Glo - ri - fy Thy
Dm7 F/G G7 C F/C C
Name in all the earth.

2.Jesus, we love Thee...
3.Spirit, we love Thee...

Bind Us Together

B.G.
Bob Gillman
F Gm7 Am7
Bind us to-ge-ther Lord, bind us to-
Dm7 Gm7 C7 F
ge-ther with cords that can-not be bro—
Gm7/C F Gm7 Am7
ken, bind us to-ge-ther, Lord, bind us to-
Dm7 Gm7 C7 F Fine
ge-ther, bind us to-ge-ther with love.
F Gm7 Am7 Gm7
There is on-ly one God.
F Gm7 C7 F
There is on-ly one king.
F Gm7 Am7 Gm7
There is on-ly one bo-dy
D.C. al Fine
F Gm7 C7 F Gm7/C
That is why we sing.

Sing Alleluia to the Lord

(1st 2 lines sung as echo to group 1)

Linda Stassen

Am
G
Am
F
Sing Al - le - lu - ia to the Lord.
Sing Al - le - lu - ia to the
Am
G
Am
E7
Sing Al - le - lu - ia to the Lord.
Lord.
Sing Al - le - lu - ia,
Am
G
F
C
Sing Al - le - lu - ia, sing Al - le - lu - ia,
Al - le - lu - ia,
Am
G
Am
Sing Al - le - lu - ia to the Lord.
Sing Al - le - lu - ia to the Lord.

Make up your own optional verses, i.e.:

a) Jesus is risen from the dead, etc.
b) We give thanks to God our King, etc.
c) Waiting on the Lord of Life, etc.

The Bond of Love

Words and Music by Otis Skillings

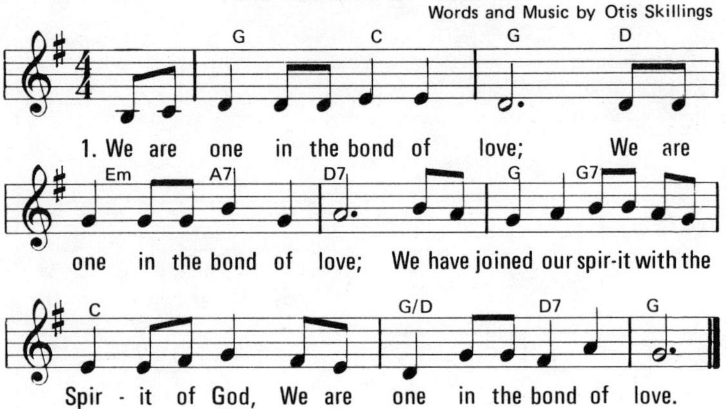
G C G D
1. We are one in the bond of love; We are
Em A7 D7 G G7
one in the bond of love; We have joined our spir-it with the
C G/D D7 G
Spir - it of God, We are one in the bond of love.

2. Let us sing now, everyone;
Let us feel His love begun;
Let us join our hands that the world will know
We are one in the bond of love.

Seek Ye First

K.L. Karen Lafferty

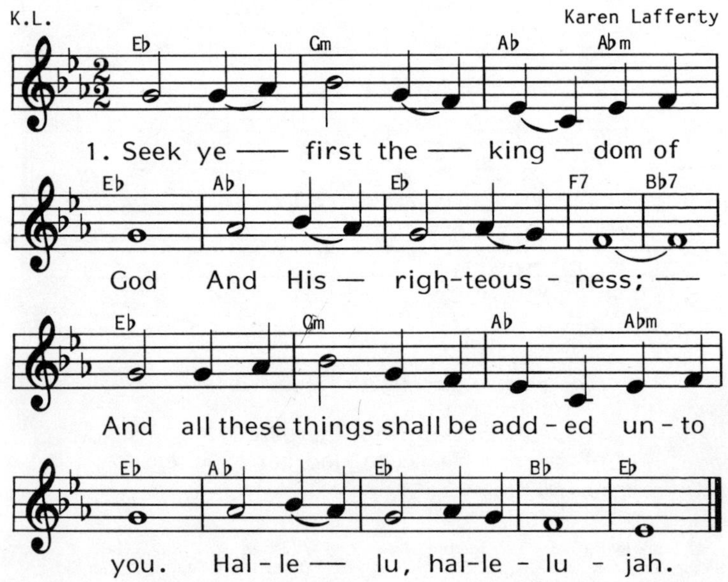
Eb Gm Ab Abm
1. Seek ye — first the — king — dom of
Eb Ab Eb F7 Bb7
God And His — righ-teous - ness; —
Eb Gm Ab Abm
And all these things shall be add - ed un - to
Eb Ab Eb Bb Eb
you. Hal - le — lu, hal-le - lu - jah.

2. Where two or three are gathered in my name,
There am I in their midst;
And whatsoever ye shall ask, I will do.
Halelu, Halelujah.

Behold What Manner of Love

Two-Part Canon

Patricia Van Tine

1.
D
G
Be - hold, what man-ner of love the Fa - ther has
D
A
D
giv - en un - to us,—— Be - hold, what
G
D
A7
man-ner of love the Fa-ther has giv - en un - to
D
2.
G
us, That we——should be
D
A
D
called the sons——of God. That
G
D
A7
D
we——should be called the sons of God.——

May sing "children of God" instead of "sons".

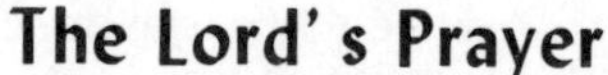
The Lord' s Prayer

J.F
John Fischer
Cmaj7 Dm7 Cmaj7 Dm7
Ho - ly Fa— ther,— hear our prayer,
Cmaj7 Dm7 Em7 Dm7
Keep us al — ways in your care;
Fmaj7 Em7 Fmaj7 G
May your king-dom come — to — us,
Cmaj7 Dm7 Em7 Dm7 Cmaj7
And may we — learn how to trust.

2. Do your will among us now,
As we here before you bow;
Give to us but what we need,
As upon your word we feed.

3. Forgive us for the things that we have not done.
When we've failed before we've yet begun;
And may we as children of Yours
Give forgiveness in return.

4. Keep us from the things that do you wrong,
When we're weak because we think we're strong;
Save us from our selfish desire;
Fill us and with your love inspire.

5. Honor, greatness belong to you,
Love and peace and mercy, too!
Praise to you again and again!
Amen.

This Is the Day

Les Garret

Psalm 118:24

4-Part Round

1
E♭
This is the day, this is the day that the
B♭7
Lord hath made, that the Lord hath made.
2
I will re - joice, I will re - joice and be
E♭
glad in it, and be glad in it.
3
A♭
E♭
This is the day that the Lord hath — made,
A♭
E♭
B♭7
I will re-joice and be glad in it.
4
E♭
This is the day, this is the
E♭/B♭
B♭7
E♭
day that the Lord hath made.

Pass It On

K.K
Kurt Kaiser
1. It on - ly takes a spark to get a fire—
go— ing,— And soon all those a-
round can warm up in its glow— ing.—
That's how it is with God's love once you've ex-
pe - ri-enced it;— You spread His love to
ev-'ry - one, You want to pass it on.—

2. What a woundrous time is spring
when all the trees are budding,
The birds begin to sing,
the flowers start their blooming.
That's how it is with God's love
once you've experienced it:
You want to sing, "It's fresh like spring";
You want to pass it on.

3. I wish for you, my friend,
this happiness I've found.
You can depend on Him;
it matters not where you're bound.
I'll shout it from the mountain top *(Hey, world!)*
I want the world to know
The Lord of love has come to me;
I want to pass it on.

Come Let Us Sing to the Lord

Tune Name: 'John Forney'

Words and Music by Jim Strathdee

Lightly
C /B Am G F G
1. Come let us sing to the Lord our — song, —
2. O thirst-y soul come — drink at the well, —
3. You dwell a-mong us and cause us to pray, And
4. Des-erts shall bloom and — moun-tains shall sing, —
Em Am G F G
We have stood si - lent - ly — too long,
God's liv-ing wa - ters — will — nev-er fail,
walk with each o - ther — fol-low-ing your way,
To the de-sire of — all — liv-ing things,
C /B Am G F G
Sure-ly the Lord de - serves our — praise To
Sure-ly the Lord will — help you to stand —
Our pre-cious broth-ers and sis-ters will grow —
Come all you crea-tures — high and — low —
Dm G Am Em F G C
joy-ful-ly thank God — for our — days.
Strength-ened and com-fort-ed by God's — hand.
In the ful-fill-ing — love they — know.
Let your — prais-es — end-less-ly flow.

We've a Story to Tell
Colin Sterne
Adapted from H. E. Nichol
We've a sto - ry to tell to the na - tions That shall turn their hearts to the right, A sto - ry of truth and mer - cy, A sto - ry of peace and light, A sto - ry of peace and light.
We've a song to be sung to the na - tions, That shall lift their hearts to the Lord; A song that shall conquer e - vil And shat - ter the spear and sword, And shat - ter the spear and sword. For the dark-ness shall
We've a mes-sage to give to the na - tions, That the Lord who reign - eth a - bove, Hath sent us His Son to save us And show us that God is love, And show us that God is love.
We've a Sav - iour to show to the na - tions, Who the path of sor - row has trod, That all of the world's great peo - ples Might come to the truth of God, Might come to the truth of God.

turn to dawn - ing, And the dawn - ing to noon - day
bright, And Christ's great king - dom shall come on
earth, The king - dom of Love and Light. A - men.
A Sunbeam
Nellie Talbot
Edwin O. Excell
A sun-beam, a sun-beam, Je-sus wants me for a sun-beam;
A sun-beam, a sun-beam, I'll be a sun-beam for Him.

Be Present at Our Table, Lord

John Cennick, 1741

Genevan Psalter, 1551
Arr. by Louis Bourgeois

Be present at our table, Lord; Be here and ev - 'ry where a-dored. These mer-cies bless and grant that we may feast in fel-low - ship with Thee.

Tallis' Canon

Thomas Ken, 1695

Thomas Tallis, 1565

*
Glo-ry to Thee, my God, this night, For all the blessings of the light;
Keep me, oh, keep me, King of Kings, Beneath Thine own Almighty wings.

* Succeeding voices enter.

Volunteer for Jesus

W.S. Brown

Chas. H. Gabriel

A vol - un-teer for Je - sus, A wor - ker true!
Oth-ers have en - list - ed, Why not you?
O why not?
Je - sus is the Cap-tain, We will nev-er fear;
Will you be en - list - ed as a vol - un - teer?

Brighten the Corner Where You Are

ina Duley Ogdon

Chas. H. Gabriel

1. Do not wait un-til some deed of great-ness you may
do, Do not wait to shed your light a - far,
To the man-y du - ties ev - er near you now be
true,

CHORUS

Bright-en the cor - ner where you are.
Bright-en the cor - ner where you are!
Shine for Je-sus where you are!

Bright-en the cor - ner where you are!

Some-one far from har-bor you may guide a - cross the

bar, the cor - ner where you are.

2. Here for all you talent you may surely find a need,
Here reflect the Bright and Morning Star,
Even from your humble hand the bread of life may feed,
Brighten the corner where you are.

Little Bells of Westminster

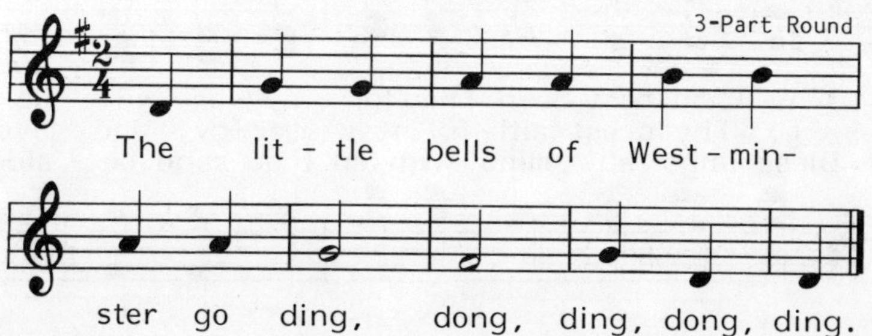
3-Part Round
The lit - tle bells of West - min-
ster go ding, dong, ding, dong, ding.

Great Is Thy Faithfulness

Thomas O. Chisolm
William M. Runyan
1. Great is Thy faith - ful-ness, O God my Fa-ther!
2. Sum-mer and win - ter and spring-time and har-vest,
3. Par-don for sin and a peace that en - dur-eth,
There is no shad - ow of turn-ing with Thee;
Sun moon and stars in their cours-es a - bove,
Thine own dear pres-ence to cheer and to guide,
Thou chang-est not, Thy com - pas-sions they fail not:
Join with all na-ture in man - i - fold wit - ness
Strength for to - day and bright hope for to - mor-row.
As Thou hast been Thou for - ev - er wilt be.
To Thy great faith-ful-ness, mer-cy, and love.
Bless - ings all mine, with ten thou-sand be - side!

Great is thy faith-ful-ness, great is Thy faith-ful-ness,
Morn-ing by morn - ing new mer - cies I see;
All I have need-ed Thy hand hath pro - vid - ed;
Great is Thy faith - ful-ness, Lord un - to me!

O, How He Loves You and Me

K.K

Kurt Kaiser

1.O how He loves you and me. O how He loves you and me; He gave His life, what more could He give; O how He loves you, O how He loves me, O how He loves you and me.
2.Je-sus to Cal-v'ry did go, His love for man-kind to show; What He did there brought hope from de-spair; O how He loves you, O how He

Nkosi Sikelel' i Afrika

Prayer for Africa

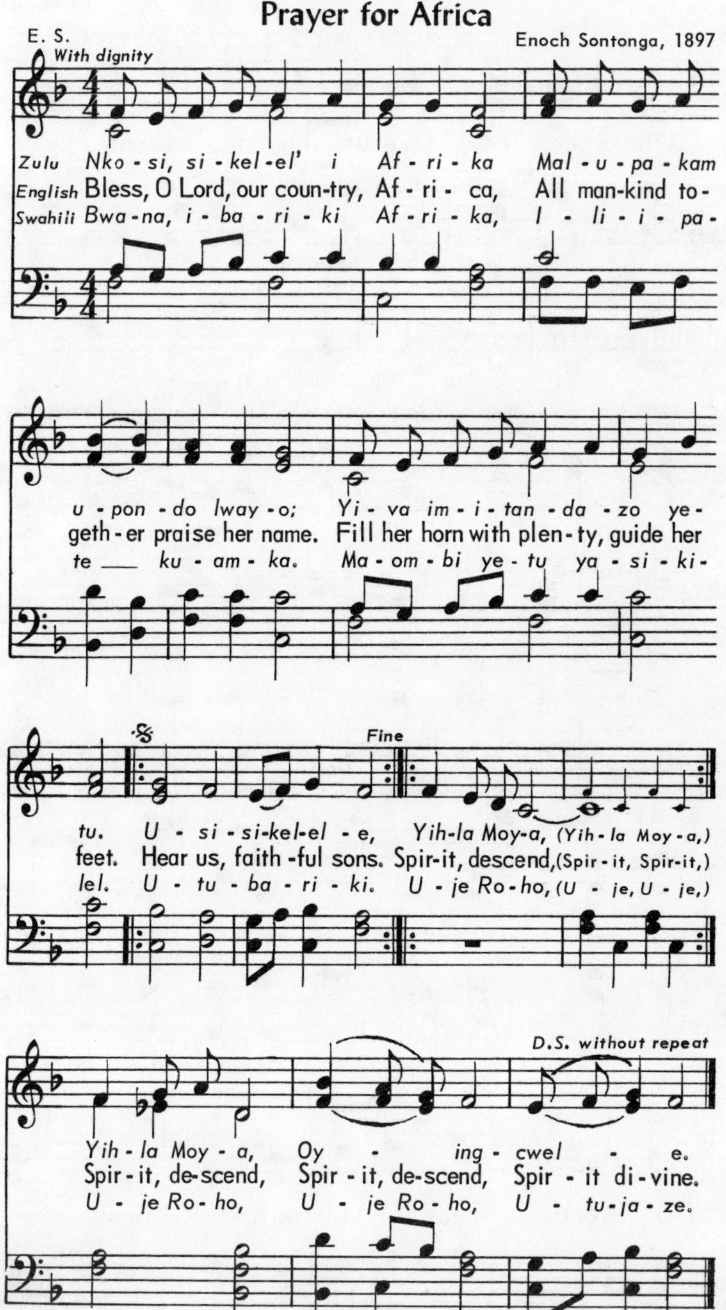
E. S.
Enoch Sontonga, 1897
With dignity
Zulu Nko - si, si - kel - el' i Af - ri - ka Mal - u - pa - kam
English Bless, O Lord, our coun-try, Af - ri - ca, All man-kind to-
Swahili Bwa - na, i - ba - ri - ki Af - ri - ka, I - li - i - pa-
u - pon - do lway - o; Yi - va im - i - tan - da - zo ye-
geth - er praise her name. Fill her horn with plen - ty, guide her
te ___ ku - am - ka. Ma - om - bi ye - tu ya - si - ki-
Fine
tu. U - si - si-kel-el - e, Yih-la Moy-a, (Yih - la Moy - a,)
feet. Hear us, faith -ful sons. Spir-it, descend,(Spir - it, Spir-it,)
lel. U - tu - ba - ri - ki. U - je Ro-ho, (U - je, U - je,)
D.S. without repeat
Yih - la Moy - a, Oy - ing - cwel - e.
Spir - it, de-scend, Spir - it, de-scend, Spir - it di - vine.
U - je Ro - ho, U - je Ro - ho, U - tu - ja - ze.

The Steadfast Love of the Lord

E.M
Edith McNeill
Bb Eb Cm7 Ab Eb
The stead-fast love of the Lord nev-er ceas-
Cm7 Ab
es. His mer - cies nev - er —— come to an
Bbsus Bb Ab Bb7
end. ——— They are new ev - 'ry morn-ing,
Gm Cm Ab Eb/Bb Eb Eb7
new ev-'ry morn-ing. Great is Thy faith-ful - ness,
Eb7 Ab Eb/Bb Bb7 Eb
O Lord. Great is Thy faith-ful - ness. ——

Rise Up, O Men

William P. Merrill | William H. Walter

1. Rise up O men of God! Have done— with lesser things; Give heart and soul and mind and strength To serve the King of kings.
2. Rise up O men of God! His king—dom tar-ries long; Bring in the day of broth-er-hood And end the night of wrong.
3. Rise up O men of God! The Church for you doth wait, Her strength un e-qual to her task: Rise up— and make her great.
4. Lift high the cross of Christ, Tread where His feet have trod; As broth-ers of the Son of man, Rise up— O men of God!

It Is Well With My Soul

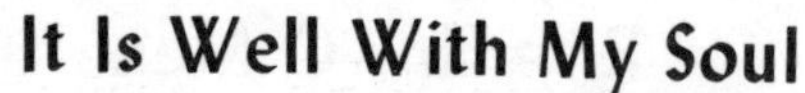

H.G. Spafford | P. P. Bliss

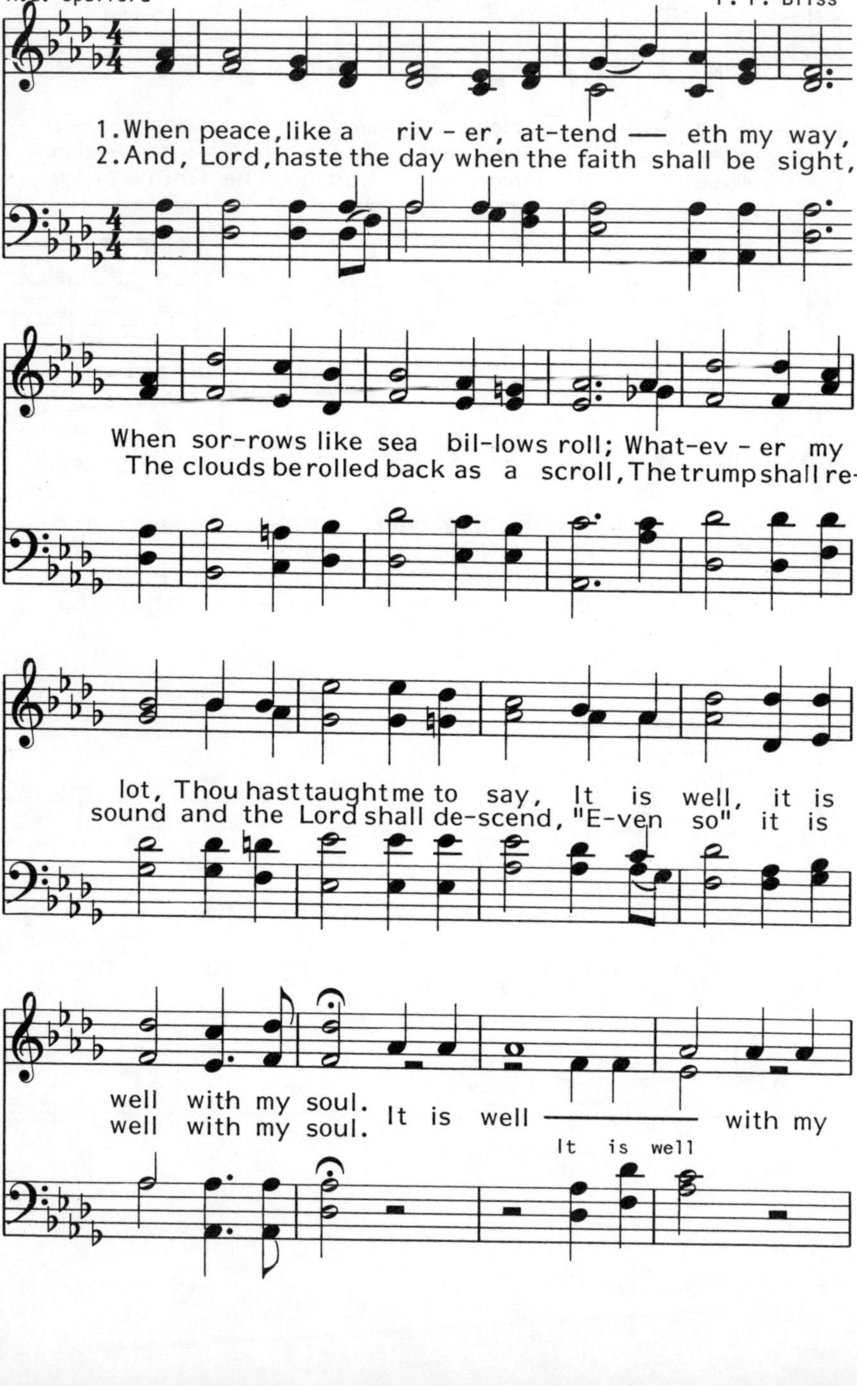
1. When peace, like a riv - er, at-tend — eth my way,
2. And, Lord, haste the day when the faith shall be sight,
When sor-rows like sea bil-lows roll; What-ev - er my
The clouds be rolled back as a scroll, The trump shall re-
lot, Thou hast taught me to say, It is well, it is
sound and the Lord shall de-scend, "E-ven so" it is
well with my soul.
well with my soul.
It is well — with my
It is well

soul, ——— It is well, it is well with my soul.
with my soul,

Lovely Evening

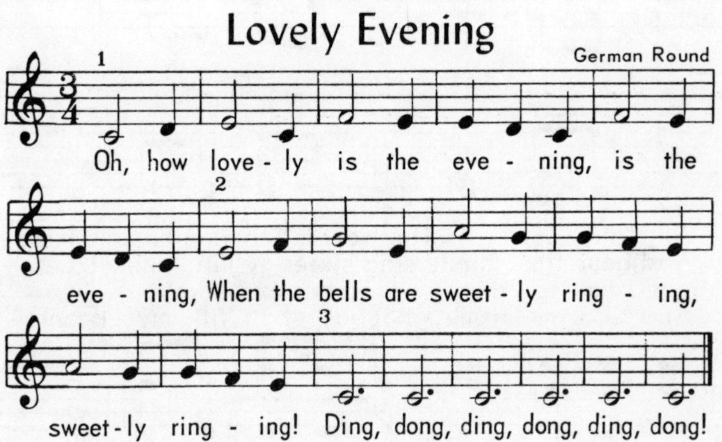
German Round
1
Oh, how love - ly is the eve - ning, is the
2
eve - ning, When the bells are sweet - ly ring - ing,
3
sweet - ly ring - ing! Ding, dong, ding, dong, ding, dong!

Hello! Hello!

Four-part Round
1 2 3 4
Hello! Hello! Hello! Hello!
We are glad to meet you, We are glad to greet you!
Hello! Hello! Hello! Hello!

From Paradology by E.O. Harbin

How Great Thou Art

S.K.H

Stuart K. Hine

1. O Lord my God! when I in awe-some won-der
2. When through the woods and for-est glades I wan-der
3. And when I think that God, His son not spar-ing,
4. When Christ shall come with shout of ac - la - ma - tion
Con - sid - er all the* worlds Thy hands have made,
And hear the birds sing sweet-ly in the trees;
Sent Him to die, I scarce can take it in;
And take me home, what joy shall fill my heart!
I see the stars, I hear the* roll - ing thun - der,
When I look down from loft-y moun-tain gran - deur
That on the cross, my bur-den glad-ly bear - ing,
Then I shall bow in hum-ble a - dor - a - tion,

*Author's original words are "works" and "mighty".

Thy pow'r thru-out the u - ni-verse dis-played:
And hear the brook and feel the gen - tle breeze:
He bled and died to take a - way my sin:
And there pro-claim, my God, how great Thou art!
Then sings my soul, my Sav-ior God, to Thee: How great Thou
art, How great Thou art!—Then sings my soul, my Sav-ior
God to Thee:—How great Thou art, — How great Thou art!—

Victory in Jesus

E.M.B. Eugene M. Bartlett, Sr.

1. I heard an old, old sto - ry, how a Sav-ior came from glo - ry, How He gave His life on Cal-va-ry to save a wretch like me; I heard a-bout His groan-ing, of His pre-cious blood's a - ton-ing, Then I re-pen-ted
2. I heard a-bout His heal - ing, of His cleans-ing pow'r re-veal - ing, How He made the lame to walk a-gain and caused the blind to see; And then I cried, "Dear Je - sus, come and heal my bro - ken spi-rit, And some-how Je-sus
3. I heard a-bout a man-sion He has built for me in glo - ry, And I heard a-bout the streets of gold be-yond the crys-tal sea; A-bout the an - gels sing-ing, and the old re-demp - tion sto-ry, And some sweet day I'll

of my sins and won the vic-to - ry.
came and bro't to me the vic-to - ry. O vic-to-ry in
sing up there the song of vic-to - ry.
Je-sus, my Sav-ior for - ev-er, He sought me and
bought me with His re-deem-ing blood; He loved me ere
I knew Him, and all my love is due Him, He
plunged me to vic-to-ry be-neath the cleans-ing flood.

Key to: F
Fairest Lord Jesus
CRUSADER'S HYMN
German, 17th Century
Silesian Folk Tune
1. Fair-est Lord Je - sus, Rul - er of all na - ture,
2. Fair are the mead - ows, Fair-er still the wood-lands,
3. Fair is the sun - shine, Fair-er still the moon - light,
O thou of God and man the son,
Robed in the bloom - ing garb of spring:
And all the twink - ling star - ry host:
Thee will I cher - ish, Thee will I hon - or, Thou
Je - sus is fair - er, Je - sus is pur - er, Who
Je-sus shines bright - er, Je-sus shines pur - er, Than
my soul's glo - ry, joy and crown.
makes the woe - ful heart to sing.
all the an - gels heaven can boast. A-men.

Revive Us Again

Wm. P. MacKay John J. Husband

1. We praise Thee, O God! for the Son of Thy love,
2. We praise Thee, O God! for Thy Spir-it of light,
3. All glo - ry and praise to the Lamb that was slain,
4. Re-vive us a - gain; fill each heart with Thy love;
For — Je - sus who died, and is now gone a - bove.
Who has shown us our Sav-ior, and scat-tered our night.
Who has borne all our sins, and has cleansed ev-'ry stain.
May each soul be re - kin-dled with fire from a - bove.
Hal-le - lu-jah Thine the glo-ry, Hal-le - lu-jah! A - men;
Hal-le - lu-jah Thine the glo-ry, re-vive us a - gain.

92

Lift High the Cross

G.W.Kitchin & M.R.Newbolt

Sydney H. Nicholson

Unison
Lift high the Cross,— the love of Christ pro-claim,— Till
all the world —— a-dore —— His sa - cred name.
Fine
Parts optional
1. Come, Chris-tians fol - low — where our Sav-ior trod,
2. Led — on their way by — this tri-um-phant sign,
3. O — Lord, once lift - ed — on this glo-rious Tree,
4. Set — up Thy throne, that earth's de-spair may cease
5. For — Thy blest Cross which doth for all a - tone,
Our — King vic — to - rious, Christ, the Son of God.
The — hosts of — God in con-qu'ring ranks com-bine.
As — Thou hast — prom-ised, draw men un-to Thee.
Be — neath the — shad - ow of it's heal-ing peace.
Cre — a - tion's — prais - es rise be-fore Thy throne.
D.C.

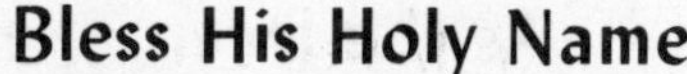
Bless His Holy Name

A.C. after Ps.103

Andrae Crouch

Bless the Lord, O my soul, and all

that is with - in me, Bless His ho——

ly—— Name.

Fine

He has done great

things,— He has done great things, He has

done great things, Bless His ho - ly Name.

D.C. al Fine

As the Deer

M.N. Martin Nystrom

As the deer pant-eth for the wa-ter, so my
soul long-eth af - ter Thee; You a-lone are my
heart's de-sire, and I long to wor —— ship
Thee You a-lone are my strength my shield, to
You a-lone may my spi - rit yield;– You a-lone

are my heart's de-sire, — and I long to wor - ship Thee.

Spirit of the Living God

E
A
E
A
1. Spir-it of the liv-ing God, fall a-fresh
B7
E
A
on me, Spir-it of the liv-ing God,
E
A
B7
E
A
E
fall a-fresh on me. Melt me, Mold me,
F#
B
A
E
Fill me, Use me. — Spir-it of the
A
E
A
B7
E
liv - ing God, fall a-fresh on me.

2. Sing "us" instead of "me".

Count Your Blessings

Rev. Johnson Oatman, Jr. E. O. Excell

1. When up-on life's bil-lows you are tem-pest tossed.
2. Are you ev-er bur-dened with a load of care?
When you are dis-cour-aged think-ing all is lost,
Does the cross seem heav-y you are called to bear?
Count your man-y bless-ings name them one by one,
Count your man-y bless-ings ev-'ry doubt will fly,
And it will sur-prise you what the Lord hath done.
And you will be sing-ing as the days go by.
CHORUS
Count your bless-ings, name them one by one;
Count your man-y bless-ings, name them one by one;

Count your bless-ings, see what God hath done;
Count your man - y bless - ings, See what God hath done;

rit.

Count your bless-ings, Name them one by one;
Count your man-y bless-ings,

a tempo

Count your man-y bless-ings, see what God hath done.

3. When you look at others with their lands and gold,
Think that Christ has promised you His wealth untold;
Count your many blessings, money cannot buy
Your reward in Heaven, nor your home on high.

4. So, amid the conflict, whether great or small,
Do not be discouraged, God is over all;
Count your many blessings, angels will attend,
Help and comfort give you to your journey's end.

To Ope Their Trunks

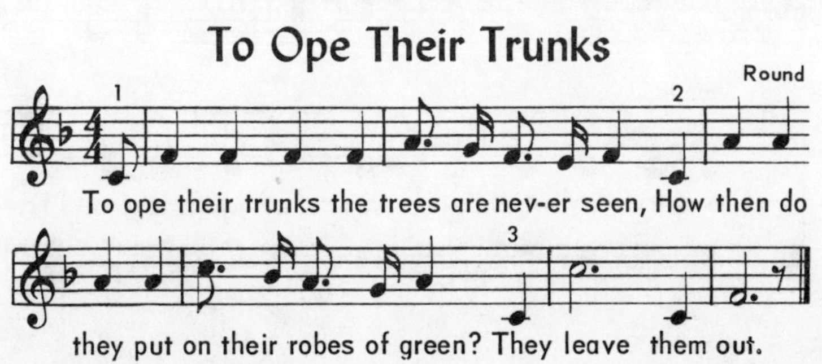
Round
1
2
3
To ope their trunks the trees are nev-er seen, How then do
they put on their robes of green? They leave them out.

Onward, Christian Soldiers

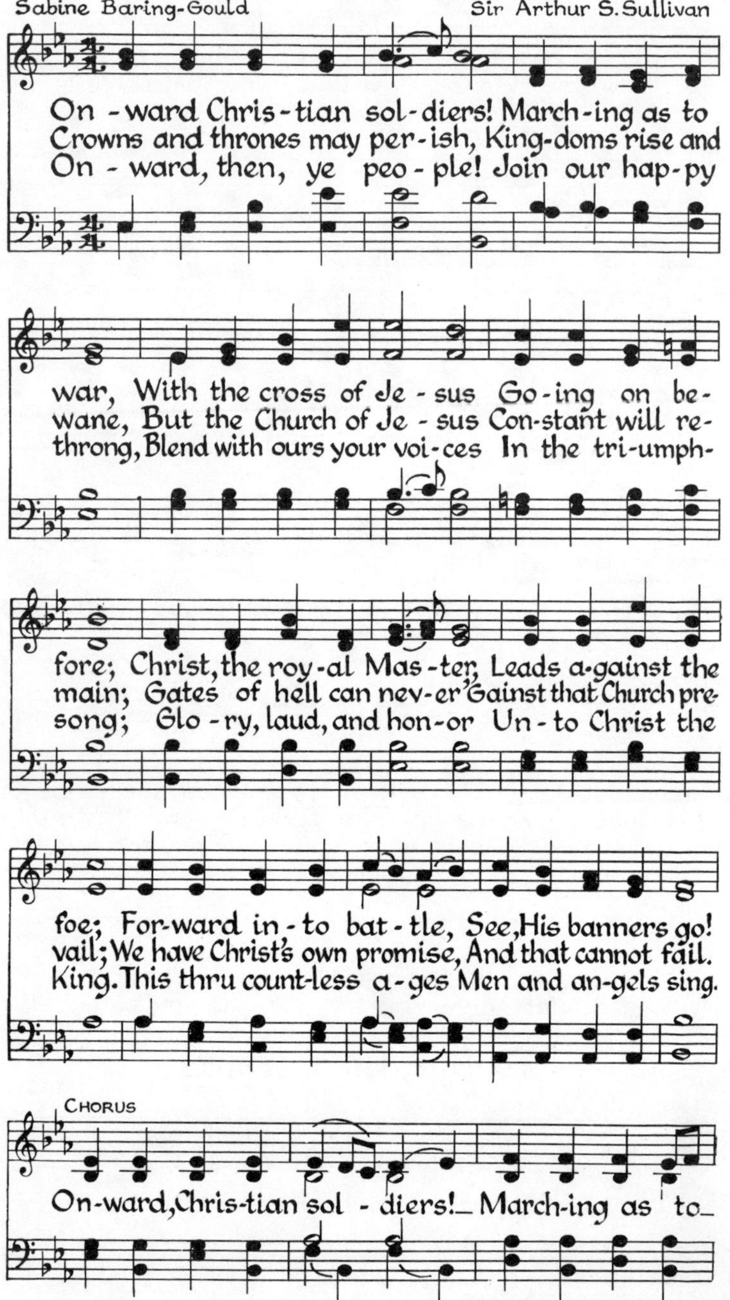
Sabine Baring-Gould
Sir Arthur S. Sullivan
On - ward Chris - tian sol - diers! March - ing as to war, With the cross of Je - sus Go - ing on be - fore; Christ, the roy - al Mas - ter, Leads a - gainst the foe; For - ward in - to bat - tle, See, His banners go!
Crowns and thrones may per - ish, King - doms rise and wane, But the Church of Je - sus Con - stant will re - main; Gates of hell can nev - er 'Gainst that Church pre - vail; We have Christ's own promise, And that cannot fail.
On - ward, then, ye peo - ple! Join our hap - py throng, Blend with ours your voi - ces In the tri - umph - song; Glo - ry, laud, and hon - or Un - to Christ the King. This thru count - less a - ges Men and an - gels sing.
CHORUS
On - ward, Chris - tian sol - diers! March - ing as to

war, With the cross of Je-sus go-ing on be-fore.

Blest Be the Tie That Binds

DENNIS

John Fawcett

In moderate time

Hans G. Naegeli
Arr. by Lowell Mason

Blest be — the tie — that binds Our hearts — in
Be - fore — our Fa-ther's throne We pour — our
We share — each oth - er's woes, Each oth - er's
When we — are called — to part, It gives — us

Chris - tian love: The fel - low-ship — of kin-dred
ar - dent prayers; Our fears, our hopes, our aims are
bur - dens bear, And of - ten for — each oth - er
in - ward pain; But we — shall still — be joined in

minds — Is like — to that — a-bove.
one, — Our com - forts and — our cares.
flows — The sym - pa-thiz - ing tear.
heart, — And hope — to meet — a-gain. A - men.

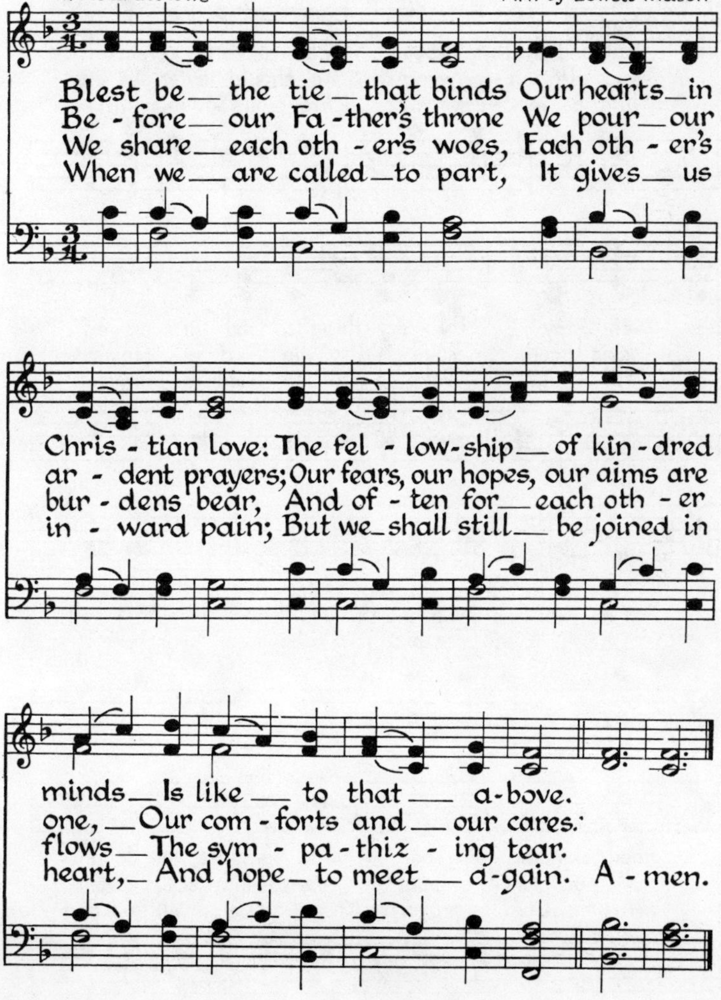

What a Friend
Joseph Scriven, 1820-1886
ERIE.
Charles C. Converse, 1832-1918
In moderate time
1. What a friend we have in Je - sus All our sins and griefs to bear; What a priv - i - lege to car - ry Ev - ery - thing to God in prayer!
2. Have we tri - als and temp - ta - tions? Is there trou - ble an - y - where? We should nev - er be dis - cour - aged; Take it to the Lord in prayer.
3. Are we weak and heav - y - la - den, Cum - bered with a load of care? Pre - cious Sav - iour, still our ref - uge; Take it to the Lord in prayer.
O what peace we oft - en for - feit, O what need - less pain we bear, All be - cause we do not
Can we find a friend so faith - ful, Who will all our sor - rows share? Je - sus knows our ev - ery
Do thy friends de - spise, for - sake thee? Take it to the Lord in prayer; Then God's arms will take and

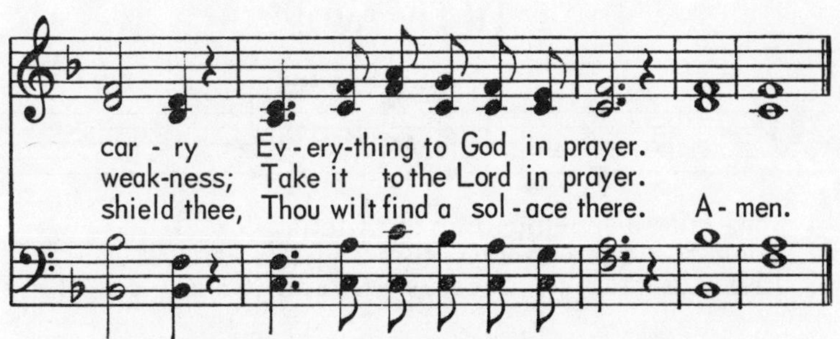
car - ry Ev-ery-thing to God in prayer.
weak-ness; Take it to the Lord in prayer.
shield thee, Thou wilt find a sol-ace there. A-men.

Morning Has Broken

Eleanor Farjeon

Gaelic Melody

C
Dm
G
1. Mor-ning has bro - ken like the first
F
C
Em
Am
mor - ning, Black-bird has spo - ken
Dsus
D
G
C
F
like the first bird. Praise for the sing-
C
Am
D
G
ing, Praise for the morn - ing, Praise for them
C
F
G7
C
F
C
spring-ing fresh from the word.

2. Sweet the rain's new fall, sunlit from heaven.
Like the first dew fall on the first grass.
Praise for the sweetness of the wet garden,
Sprung in completeness where His feet pass.

3. Mine is the sunlight, mine is the morning,
Born of the one light Eden saw play.
Praise with elation, praise every morning,
God's recreation of the new day.

I'll Fly Away

A.E.B.
Albert E. Brumley
1. Some glad morn-ing when this life is o'er,
2. When the shad-ows of this life have gone,
3. Just a few more wea-ry days and then,
I'll fly a-way
fly a-way;
fly a-way;
To a home on God's ce-les-tial shore,
Like a bird from pri-son bars has flown,
To a land where joys shall ne-ver end,
I'll fly a-way,
fly a-way,
fly a-way.
I'll fly a-way, O glo-ry, I'll fly a-
fly a-way,
fly a-way,

way; ——— When I die, hal-le - lu-jah, by and
in the morn-ing;

by, —— I'll ——— fly a - way. ———
fly a-way fly a - way.

He Is Lord

Gm7
C7
F
B♭
He is Lord! ——— He is Lord! ——
F
Dm
G7
—— He is ris - en from the dead and He is
Gm7
C7
F
Am
Lord! ——— Ev - 'ry knee shall
F7
E♭/F
F7
B♭
B♭m
bow, ev - 'ry tongue con - fess that
F/C
Am/C
C7
F
B♭
F
Je - sus Christ is Lord! ———

They That Wait On the Lord

Isaiah 40:31
S.H.

Stuart Hamblen

They that wait — up-on the Lord — shall re - new
their strength; — They shall mount up with wings — like
ea - gles; — They shall run, — and not be
wea-ry; They shall walk, — and not — faint. Teach me,

Lord, teach me, Lord, — to wait. ———

O Master, Let Me Walk

MARYTON

Washington Gladden — Henry P. Smith

1. O Mas-ter, let me walk with Thee In low-ly
2. Help me the slow of heart to move By some clear,
3. Teach me Thy pa-tience; still with Thee, In clos-er,
4. In hope that sends a shin-ing ray Far down the

paths of ser-vic e free; Tell me Thy se-cret,
win-ning word of love; Teach me the way-ward
dear-er com-pa-ny, In work that keeps faith
fu-ture's broad-ening way; In peace that on-ly

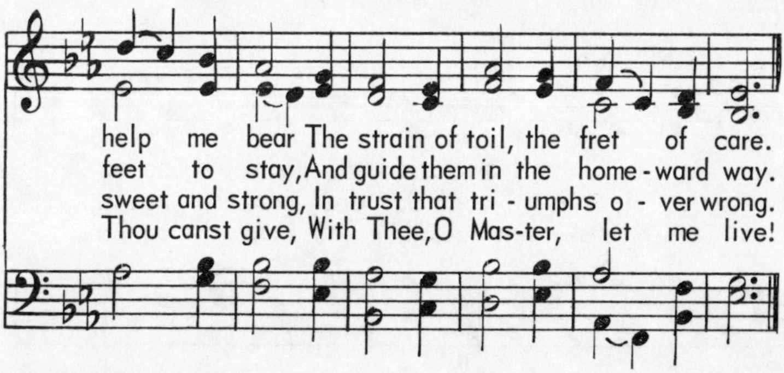

help me bear The strain of toil, the fret of care.
feet to stay, And guide them in the home-ward way.
sweet and strong, In trust that tri-umphs o-ver wrong.
Thou canst give, With Thee, O Mas-ter, let me live!

Mine Eyes Have Seen the Glory

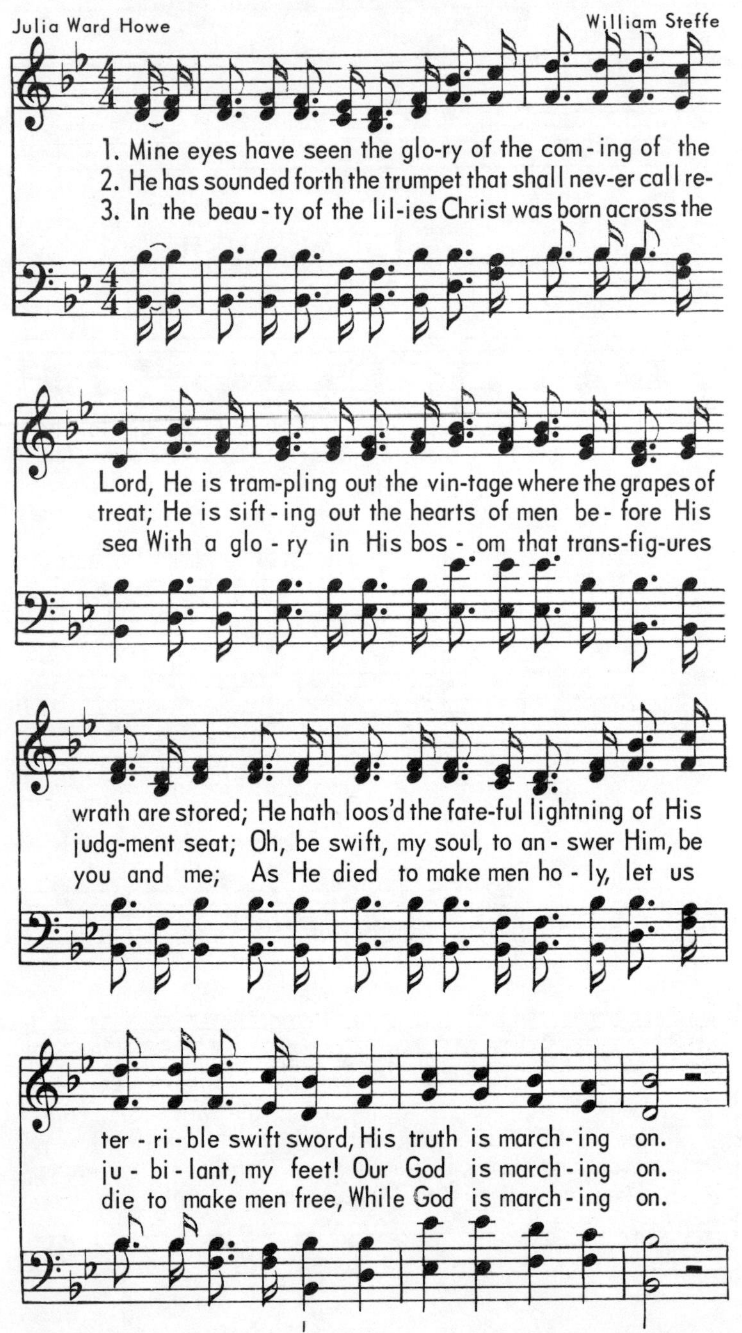
Julia Ward Howe
William Steffe
1. Mine eyes have seen the glo-ry of the com - ing of the Lord, He is tram-pling out the vin-tage where the grapes of wrath are stored; He hath loos'd the fate-ful lightning of His ter - ri - ble swift sword, His truth is march - ing on.
2. He has sounded forth the trumpet that shall nev-er call re-treat; He is sift - ing out the hearts of men be - fore His judg-ment seat; Oh, be swift, my soul, to an - swer Him, be ju - bi - lant, my feet! Our God is march - ing on.
3. In the beau - ty of the lil-ies Christ was born across the sea With a glo - ry in His bos - om that trans-fig-ures you and me; As He died to make men ho - ly, let us die to make men free, While God is march - ing on.

Glo-ry, glo-ry, hal-le-lu-jah! Glo-ry, glo-ry, hal-le-lu-jah!
Glo-ry, glo-ry, hal-le-lu-jah! His truth is marching on.

Rejoice in the Lord Always

Philippians 4:4

4-Part Canon
Traditional

Re-joice in the Lord — al — ways, a-
gain I say, re-joice! Re-joice in the Lord
al — ways, a-gain I say, re-joice! Re-
joice, re-joice, a-gain I say re-joice! Re-
joice, re-joice, a-gain I say re-joice

I Surrender All

Judson W. Van de Venter

Winfield S. Weeden

1. All to Jesus I surrender, All to Him I freely give; I will ever love and trust Him In His presence daily live.
2. All to Jesus I surrender, Humbly at His feet I bow, Worldly pleasures all forsaken, Take me Jesus, take me now.
3. All to Jesus I surrender, Make me, Savior, wholly Thine. Let me feel the Holy Spirit, Truly know that Thou art mine.
4. All to Jesus I surrender, Lord, I give myself to Thee; Fill me with Thy love and power, Let Thy blessing fall on me.
I surrender all, I surrender all,
I surrender all, I surrender all

All to Thee, my bless-ed Sav-ior, I sur-ren-der all.
Jesus Calls Us
GALILEE
Cecil F. Alexander
William H. Jude
1. Je-sus calls us o'er the tu-mult Of our life's wild rest-less sea, Day by day His sweet voice sound-eth, Say-ing: "Chris-tian, fol-low me!"
2. Je-sus calls us from the wor-ship Of the vain world's gold-en store; From each i-dol that would keep us, Say-ing: "Chris-tian, love me more!"
3. In our joys and in our sor-rows, Days of toil and hours of ease, Still He calls in cares and plea-sures, "Christian love me more than these."
4. Je-sus calls us: by Thy mer-cies, Sav-ior may we hear Thy call, Give our hearts to Thine o-be-dience Serve and love Thee best of all.

Gloria in Excelsis

Traditional French carol

Glo
ri - a in ex - cel - sis De - o,
Glo
ri - a in - ex - cel - sis De o.

Sing this great chorus all year long!

Open Our Eyes, Lord

Robert Cull
arr. David Allen
R.C.

1. O-pen our eyes, Lord — we want to see
2. O-pen our ears, Lord — and help us to
Je - sus, — to reach out and touch
lis - ten, — O - pen our eyes,
1
Him, — and say that we love Him. —
2
Lord, — we want to see Je - sus. —

He Lives

A.H.A. Alfred H. Ackley

1. I serve a ris-en Sav - ior, He's in the world to-
2. In all the world a-round me, I see His lov-ing
3. Re-joice, re-joice, O Christ-ian, lift up your voice and
day; — I know that He is liv - ing, what-
care, — And though my heart grows wea - ry I
sing — E - ter-nal hal - le - lu - jahs to
ev - er men may say; — I see His hand of
nev - er will de-spair; — I know that He is
Je - sus Christ the King! — The hope of all who
mer - cy I hear His voice of cheer, — And
lead - ing through all the storm - y blast, — The
seek Him the help of all who find, — None

just the time I need Him He's al - ways near.
day of His ap-pear-ing will come at last.
oth - er is so lov-ing, so good and kind.
He lives, — He lives, — Christ Je-sus lives to-day!
He lives,
He lives,
He walks with me and talks with me a-long life's nar-row way.
He lives, — He lives, — sal-va-tion to im-part! —
He lives
He lives
You ask me how I know He lives? He lives with-in my heart.

All Hail the Power

DIADEM

Edward Perronet, 1726-1792
Alt. by John Rippon, 1751-1836

James Ellor, 1819-1899

1. All hail the power of Je - sus' Name! Let angels prostrate
2. Ye cho - sen seed of Is - rael's race, Ye ransomed from the
3. Sin - ners, whose love can ne'er for - get The wormwood and the
4. Let ev - ery kin - dred, ev - ery tribe, On this ter - res - trial
5. O that with yon - der sa - cred throng We at His feet may
fall, Let ang - els pros - trate fall; Bring forth the roy - al
fall, Ye ran - somed from the fall; Hail Him who saves you
gall, The worm - wood and the gall, Go, spread your tro - phies
ball, On this ter - res - trial ball, To Him all maj - es -
fall, We at His feet may fall! We'll join the ev - er -
di - a - dem, And crown. . . . . Him,
by His grace, And crown. . . . . Him,
at His feet, And crown. . . . . Him,
ty as - cribe, And crown . . . . Him,
last - ing song, And crown . . . . Him,
crown Him, crown Him, crown Him, crown Him,
crown . . . .
crown Him, crown Him, crown Him, And crown Him Lord of all.
. . . . Him,

O For a Thousand Tongues

RICHMOND

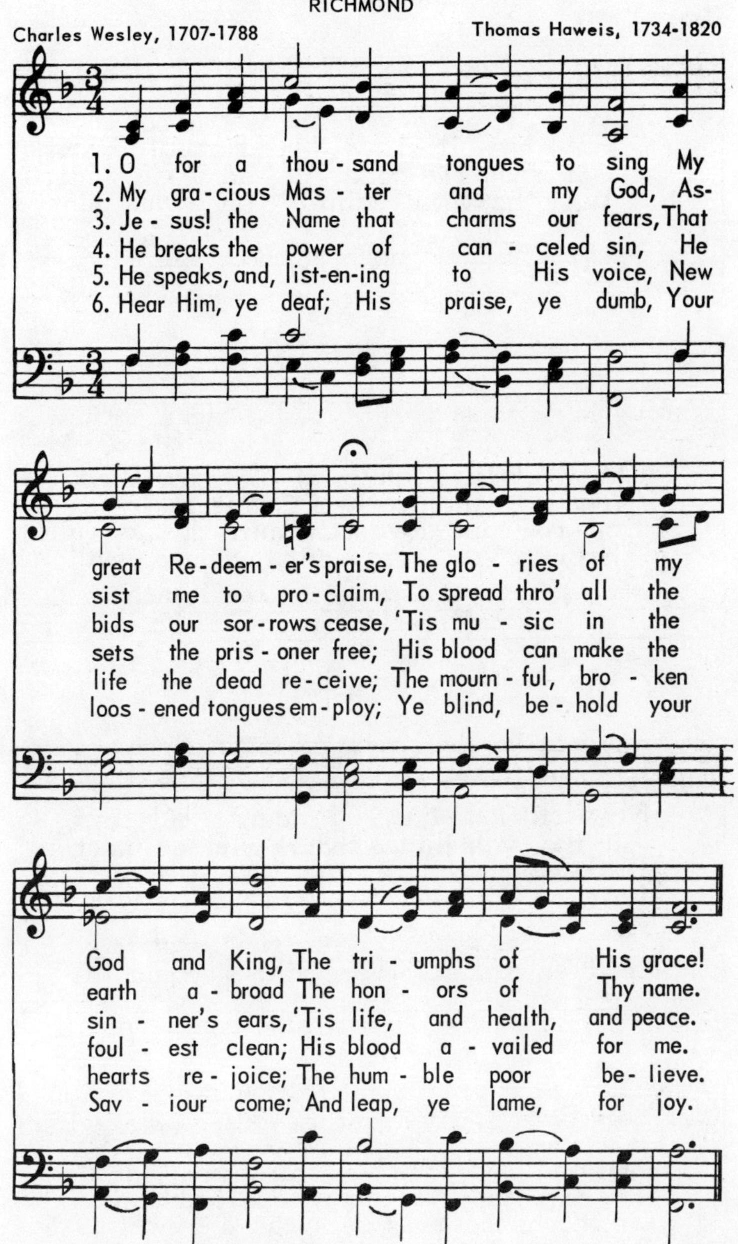
Charles Wesley, 1707-1788
Thomas Haweis, 1734-1820
1. O for a thou - sand tongues to sing My
2. My gra - cious Mas - ter and my God, As-
3. Je - sus! the Name that charms our fears, That
4. He breaks the power of can - celed sin, He
5. He speaks, and, list-en-ing to His voice, New
6. Hear Him, ye deaf; His praise, ye dumb, Your
great Re - deem - er's praise, The glo - ries of my
sist me to pro - claim, To spread thro' all the
bids our sor - rows cease, 'Tis mu - sic in the
sets the pris - oner free; His blood can make the
life the dead re - ceive; The mourn - ful, bro - ken
loos - ened tongues em - ploy; Ye blind, be - hold your
God and King, The tri - umphs of His grace!
earth a - broad The hon - ors of Thy name.
sin - ner's ears, 'Tis life, and health, and peace.
foul - est clean; His blood a - vailed for me.
hearts re - joice; The hum - ble poor be - lieve.
Sav - iour come; And leap, ye lame, for joy.

When I Survey

ROCKINGHAM

Isaac Watts — Edward Miller

When I sur-vey the won-drous cross
For-bid it, Lord, that I should boast,
See from His head, His hands, His feet,
Were the whole realm of na-ture mine,
On which the Prince of glo-ry died,
Save in the death of Christ, my God;
Sor-row and love flow min-gled down!
That were a pres-ent far too small;
My rich-est gain I count but loss,
All the vain things that charm me most
Did e'er such love and sor-row meet,
Love so a-maz-ing, so di-vine,
And pour con-tempt on all my pride.
I sac-ri-fice them to His blood.
Or thorns com-pose so rich a crown?
De-mands my soul, my life, my all. A-men.

Blessed Assurance

ASSURANCE
Fanny J. Crosby, 1820-1915
Mrs. Joseph F. Knapp, 1839-1908
1. Bless-ed as-sur-ance, Je-sus is mine! Oh, what a fore-taste of glo-ry di-vine! Heir of sal-va-tion, pur-chase of God, Born of His Spir-it, wash'd in His blood.
2. Per-fect sub-mis-sion, per-fect de-light, Vi-sions of rap-ture now burst on my sight: An-gels de-scend-ing bring from a-bove Ech-oes of mer-cy, whis-pers of love.
3. Per-fect sub-mis-sion, all is at rest, I in my Sav-iour am hap-py and blest: Watch-ing and wait-ing, look-ing a-bove Fill'd with His good-ness, lost in His love.
Refrain
This is my sto-ry, this is my song, Prais-ing my Sav-iour all the day long; This is my sto-ry, this is my song, Prais-ing my Sav-iour all the day long.

We Gather Together
Tr. by Theodore Baker
KREMSER
Netherlands, 1625
We gath - er to - geth - er to ask the Lord's
Be - side us to guide us, our God with us
We all do ex - toll Thee, Thou Lead - er tri-
bless - ing; He chas - tens and has - tens His
join - ing, Or - dain - ing, main - tain - ing His
um - phant, And pray that Thou still our De-
will to make known; The wick-ed op-press-ing now
king - dom di - vine; So from the be-gin-ning the
fen - der wilt be. Let Thy con-gre-ga-tion es-
cease from dis-tress-ing, Sing prais - es to His
fight we were win-ning: Thou, Lord, wast at our
cape trib - u - la - tion: Thy Name be ev-er
Name: He for-gets not His own.
side, all glo - ry be Thine!
praised! O Lord, make us free! A-men.

Where Cross the Crowded Ways

GERMANY
Frank Mason North, 1903
Gardiner's *Sacred Melodies*, 1815
1. Where cross the crowd-ed ways_of life, Where sound the
2. In haunts of wretch-ed-ness_and need, On shad-owed
3. From ten-der child-hood's help-less-ness, From woman's
cries of race_and clan, A-bove the noise_of
thresholds dark_with fears, From paths where hide the
grief, man's bur-dened toil, From fam-ished souls, from
self-ish strife, We hear Thy voice, O Son_of man.
lures of greed, We catch the vis-ion of_Thy tears.
sor-row's stress, Thy heart has nev-er known re-coil.

4. O Master, from the mountain-side
Make haste to heal these hearts of pain;
Among these restless throngs abide,
O tread the city streets again,

5. Till sons of men shall learn Thy love,
And follow where Thy feet have trod;
Till glorious from Thy heaven above
Shall come the City of our God.

I Love to Tell the Story

HANKEY

Katherine Hankey, 1834-1911 William G. Fischer, 1835-1910

1. I love to tell the sto - ry Of un-seen things a - bove, Of Je - sus and His glo - ry, Of Je - sus and His love. I love to tell the sto - ry, Be - cause I know 'tis true; It sat - is-
2. I love to tell the sto - ry; More won-der ful it seems Than all the gold - en fan-cies Of all our gold - en dreams. I love to tell the sto - ry, It did so much for me; And that is
3. I love to tell the sto - ry, For those who know it best Seem hun-ger-ing and thirst-ing To hear it like the rest. And when, in scenes of glo - ry, I sing the new, new song, 'Twill be the

fies my long-ings As noth-ing else can do.
just the rea - son I tell it now to thee.
old, old sto - ry That I have loved so long.
Refrain
I love to tell the sto-ry, 'Twill be my theme in glo-ry,
To tell the old, old sto-ry Of Je-sus and His love.
F Gm C7 F 2 Gm
1
1. Fa - ther, I a - dore you; lay my life be -
2. Je - sus,
3. Spir - it,

Father, I Adore You

Words and Music by Terrye Coelho

C F 3 Gm C7 F

fore you. How I love you!

O Zion, Haste

Mary A. Thomson
James Walch
1. O Zion, haste, thy mis - sion high ful-fill - ing, To
2. Pro-claim to ev - 'ry peo-ple, tongue, and na-tion
3. Give of thy sons to bear the mes-sage glo-rious,
To tell to all the world that God is light;
That God in whom they live and move is love;
Give of thy wealth to speed them on their way;
That He who made all na-tions is not wil - ling
Tell how He stooped to save His lost cre - a - tion,
Pour out thy soul for them in prayer vic - to-rious,
One soul should pe - rish, lost in shades of night.
And died on earth that man might live a - bove.
And haste the com-ing of the glo-rious day.

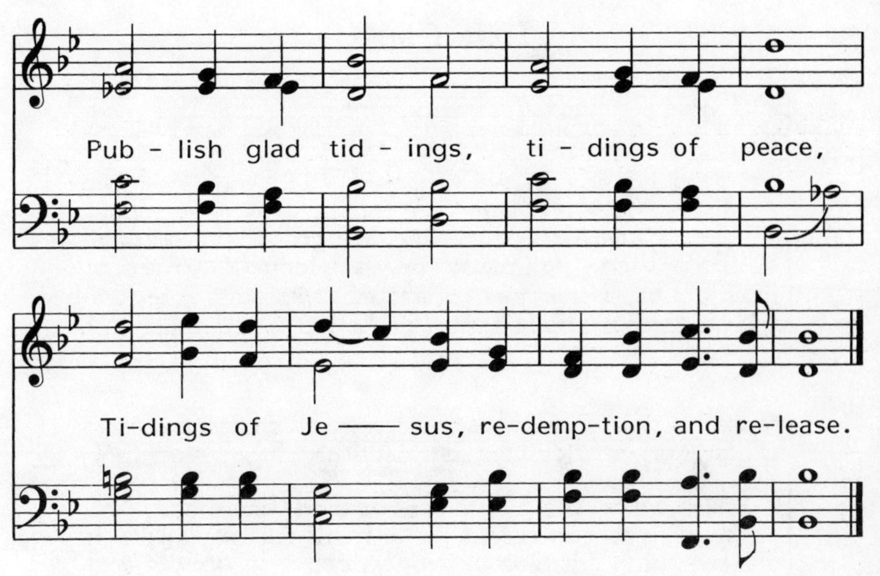
Pub - lish glad tid - ings, ti - dings of peace,
Ti-dings of Je —— sus, re-demp-tion, and re-lease.

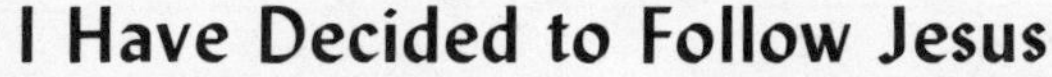

I Have Decided to Follow Jesus

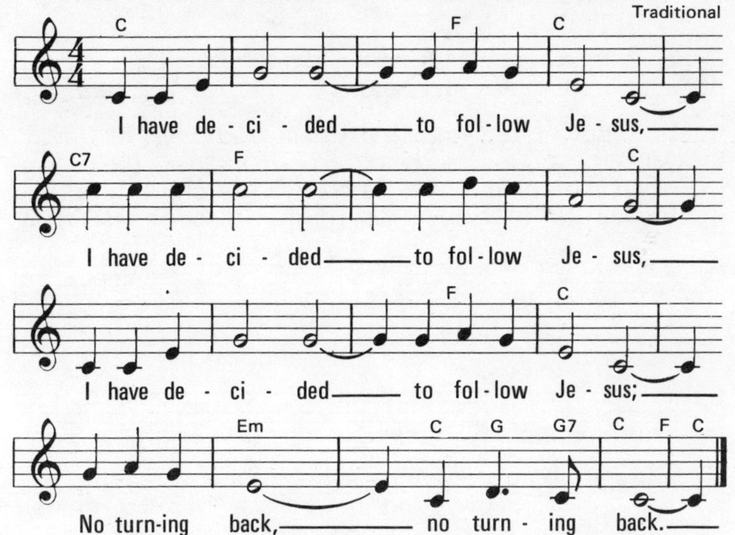
Traditional
C F C
I have de - ci - ded —— to fol - low Je - sus, ——
C7 F C
I have de - ci - ded —— to fol - low Je - sus, ——
F C
I have de - ci - ded —— to fol - low Je - sus; ——
Em C G G7 C F C
No turn-ing back, —— no turn - ing back. ——

2. Though I may wonder, still I will follow; (3x)
   No lookin' back, no lookin' back!

3. The world around me, the Lord before me, (3x)
   I'm movin' on, I'm movin' on!

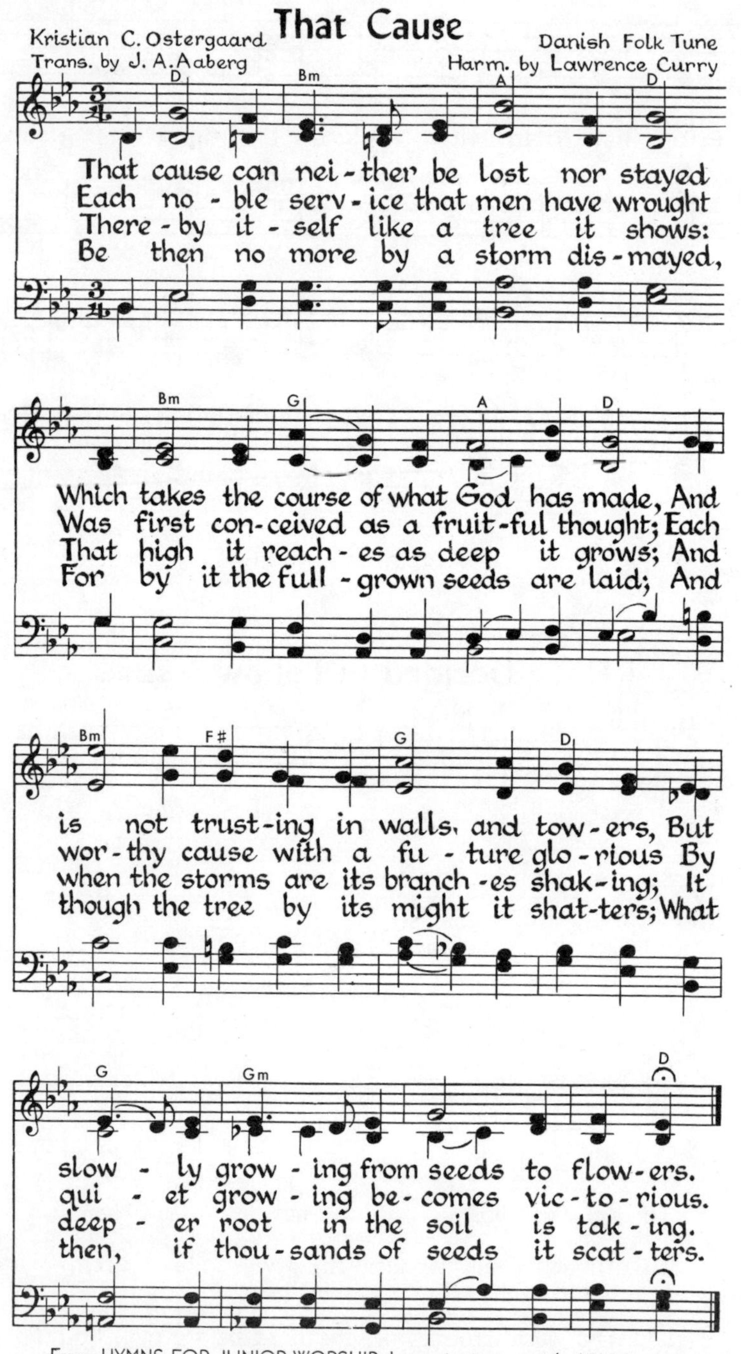
That Cause
Kristian C. Ostergaard
Trans. by J. A. Aaberg
Danish Folk Tune
Harm. by Lawrence Curry
D Bm A D
That cause can nei - ther be lost nor stayed
Each no - ble serv - ice that men have wrought
There - by it - self like a tree it shows:
Be then no more by a storm dis - mayed,
Bm G A D
Which takes the course of what God has made, And
Was first con - ceived as a fruit - ful thought; Each
That high it reach - es as deep it grows; And
For by it the full - grown seeds are laid; And
Bm F# G D
is not trust - ing in walls and tow - ers, But
wor - thy cause with a fu - ture glo - rious By
when the storms are its branch - es shak - ing; It
though the tree by its might it shat - ters; What
G Gm D
slow - ly grow - ing from seeds to flow - ers.
qui - et grow - ing be - comes vic - to - rious.
deep - er root in the soil is tak - ing.
then, if thou - sands of seeds it scat - ters.

Deck the Hall

Old Welsh Carol

Deck the hall with boughs of hol-ly,
See the blaz-ing yule be-fore us, Fa la la la la la
Fast a-way the old year pas-ses,
'Tis the sea-son to be jol-ly,
la la la. Strike the harp and join the cho-rus, Fa la la la
Hail the new, ye lads and las-ses,
Don we now our gay ap-par-el,
la la la la la. Fol-low me in mer-ry meas-ure,
Sing we joy-ous all to-geth-er,
Troll the an-cient
Fa la la la la la la la la. While I tell of
Heed-less of the
yule-tide car-ol,
yule-tide treas-ure. Fa la la la la la la la la.
wind and weath-er,

Amazing Grace

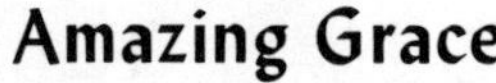

John Newton | Early American

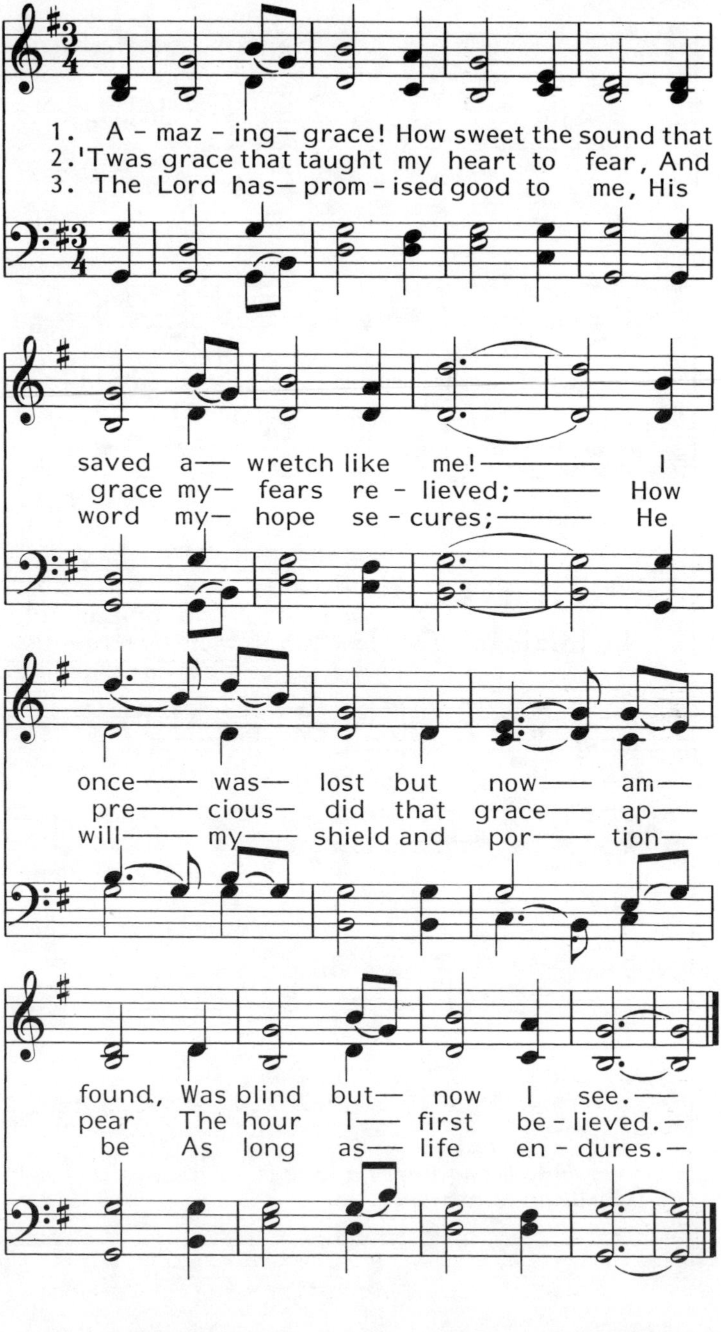
1. A - maz - ing— grace! How sweet the sound that saved a— wretch like me!— I once— was— lost but now— am— found, Was blind but— now I see.—
2.'Twas grace that taught my heart to fear, And grace my— fears re - lieved;— How pre— cious— did that grace— ap— pear The hour I— first be - lieved.—
3. The Lord has— prom - ised good to me, His word my— hope se - cures;— He will— my— shield and por— tion— be As long as— life en - dures.—

4. Through many dangers, toils and snares,
I have already come;
'Tis grace that brought me safe thus far,
And grace will lead me home.

5. When we've been here ten thousand years,
Bright shining as the sun,
We've no less time to sings God's praise,
Than when we'd first begun.

-5th verse by John P. Rees-

Alleluia

by Jerry Sinclair

G C Am
Al - le - lu - ia, al - le - lu - ia,
D7 G
al - le - lu - ia, al - le - lu - ia. Al - le
G C Am D7
lu - ia, al - le - lu - ia al - le - lu - ia,
1 Am7 G 2 C G
al - le - lu - ia. lu - ia.

2. He's my Savior.
3. I will praise Him.

(Make up your own.)

Band of Neighbors

E♭ 1 2 3
As a band of neigh-bors joined, one in heart and
one in mind, Peace and safe-ty we shall find.

Church in the Wildwood

W. S. P.
William S. Pitts
There's a church in the val-ley by the wild-wood, No
How_ sweet on a bright Sabbath morn-ing To
lov-li-er place in the dale; No_ spot is so dear to my
list to the clear ringing bell; Its_ tones so sweet-ly are
Fine
child-hood As the lit-tle brown church in the vale._
call - ing, O_ come_ to the church in the vale._
rit.
a tempo
Come to the church in the wild -
O_ come, come, come, come, come, come, come, come, come, come,
wood, O come to the church in the dale;
D.S.
come, come, come, come, come, come, come, come, come, No_

O, How I Love Jesus

Frederick Whitfield | American Melody

G
1. There is a name — I love to hear, I
D | G
love to sing — its worth; — It sounds like
D7
mu — sic in my ear, The sweet — est
G
name on earth.

CHORUS
O, how I love Je - sus,
D7 | G
O, how I love Je - sus —
O, how I love
D7 | G
Je - sus Be-cause — He first loved me. —

2. It tells me of a Savior's love,
Who died to set me free;
It tells me of His precious blood,
The sinner's perfect plea.

3. It tells me of One whose loving heart
Can feel my deepest woe,
Who in each sorrow bears a part
That none can bear below.

For Health and Strength

1 G 2 D7 G 3 D7 G 4 D7 G
For health and strength and dai-ly food, we praise Thy name, O Lord!

Tell Me the Story of Jesus

Fanny J. Crosby

John R. Sweney

1. Tell me the sto - ry of Je - sus, Write on my
2. Fast - ing a-lone in the des - ert, Tell of the
3. Tell of the cross where they nailed Him, Writh-ing in
Refrain: Tell me the sto - ry of Je - sus, Write on my
heart ev-'ry word; Tell me the sto - ry most
days that are past, How for our sins He was
an-guish and pain; Tell of the grave where they
heart ev-'ry word; Tell me the sto-ry most
Fine
pre - cious, Sweet - est that ev - er was heard.
tempt - ted, Yet was tri - um-phant at last.
laid Him, Tell how He liv - eth a - gain.
pre - cious, Sweet - est that ev - er was heard.
Tell how the an-gels in cho - rus Sang as they
Tell of the years of His la - bor, Tell of the
Love in that sto - ry so ten - der, Clear - er than

wel-comed His birth, "Glo - ry to God in the
sor - row He bore, He was de-spised and af-
ev - er I see: Stay, let me weep while you

D.C. for refrain

high - est! Peace and good ti — dings to earth." —
flict - ed, Home-less re-ject — ed and poor. —
whis - per, Love paid the ran — some for me. —

Now the Day Is Over

MERRIAL

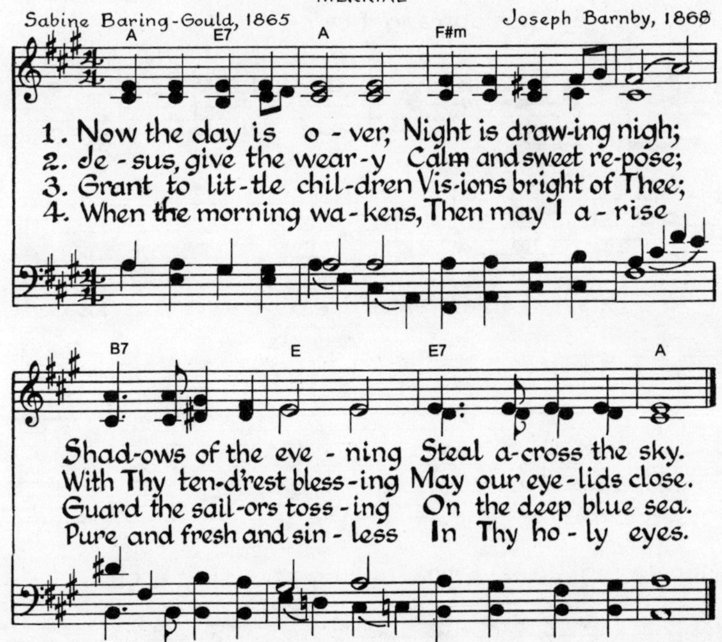
Sabine Baring-Gould, 1865
Joseph Barnby, 1868
A E7 A F#m
1. Now the day is o - ver, Night is draw-ing nigh;
2. Je - sus, give the wear-y Calm and sweet re-pose;
3. Grant to lit-tle chil-dren Vis-ions bright of Thee;
4. When the morning wa-kens, Then may I a - rise
B7 E E7 A
Shad-ows of the eve - ning Steal a-cross the sky.
With Thy ten-d'rest bless-ing May our eye-lids close.
Guard the sail-ors toss - ing On the deep blue sea.
Pure and fresh and sin - less In Thy ho - ly eyes.

He Keeps Me Singing

L.B.B. Luther B. Bridgers

1. There's with-in my heart a mel - o - dy Je-sus whis-pers
sweet and low—"Fear not, I am with thee, peace be still,"
In all of life's ebb and flow.
REFRAIN
Je - sus, Je - sus,
Je - sus, sweet-est name I know,
Fills my ev - 'ry
long - ing, Keeps me sing-ing as I go.

2. All my life was wrecked by sin and strife,
Discord filled my heart with pain;
Jesus swept across the broken strings,
Stirred the slumbering chords again.

3. Feasting on the riches of His grace,
Resting 'neath His shelterting wing,
Always looking on His smiling face,
That is why I shout and sing.

4. Though sometimes He leads through waters deep,
Trials fall across the way,
Though sometimes the path seems rough and steep,
See His footprints all the way.

5. Soon He's coming back to welcome me,
Far beyond the starry sky;
I shall wing my flight to worlds unknown,
I shall reign with Him on high.

Into My Heart

Words and Music by Harry D. Clarke

F
In - to my heart, in - to my heart, Come
C7 Bb/F F Bb F/A
in - to my heart, Lord Je - sus; Come in to-day, come
C7/G F Bb C/Bb F/A C7/G F C7 F
in to stay, Come in - to my heart, Lord Je - sus.

Additional verse (author unknown)

Out of my life, out of my life,
Shine out of my life, Lord Jesus.
Shine out today, shine out always,
Shine out of my life, Lord Jesus.

Thou, O Lord, Who Through Past Ages

Helen Park Eisenberg — Franz Joseph Haydn

1. Thou, O Lord who thru past ag — es Brought thy
2. We have sav-ored songs of vic-to - ry, We have
3. Hear we now God's end-less prom - ise: If my
home-less to this — land, Led them thru much
al - so fall - en — low, Ris - ing on - ly
peo - ple, called by my name, Hum - ble selves, and
trib-u - la — tion Blessed them with a vis - ion — grand;
when in pen - i-tence Con - trite hearts a - gain we — show.
pray and seek me, Turn - ing from their wick-ed — ways,
Raise we now — in ex - al - ta - tion —
Raise we now — in a - dor - a - tion —
Then will I from heav - en hear them, For-

Praise for— thy a - bi - ding love. Thou sus-tained- us,
Praise for— thy for - giv - ing love. Thou sus-tained- us,
give their sin and heal their land. Oh, sus-tain—— us,

thou u - ni-ted us; Give we thanks to — God a - bove.
thou u - ni-ted us; Give we thanks to — God a - bove.
Oh, u - nite — us, As a — gain we — seek Thy face.

God Is So Good

Traditional
F C7 F
1. God is so good; God is so good;
2. God meets my needs; God meets my needs;
3. God an - swers prayer; God an - swers prayer;
B♭ F C7 F
God is so good; God is good to me.
God meets my needs; God is good to me.
God an - swers prayer; God is good to me.

His Name Is Wonderful

A.M.
Audrey Mieir
His name is Won-der-ful, His name is Won-der-ful,
His name is Won-der-ful Je - sus my Lord;
He is the migh-ty King, Mas - ter of ev-'ry-thing,
His name is Won-der-ful, Je - sus my Lord. He's the great
Shep-herd, the Rock of all a - ges, Al-might-y God is

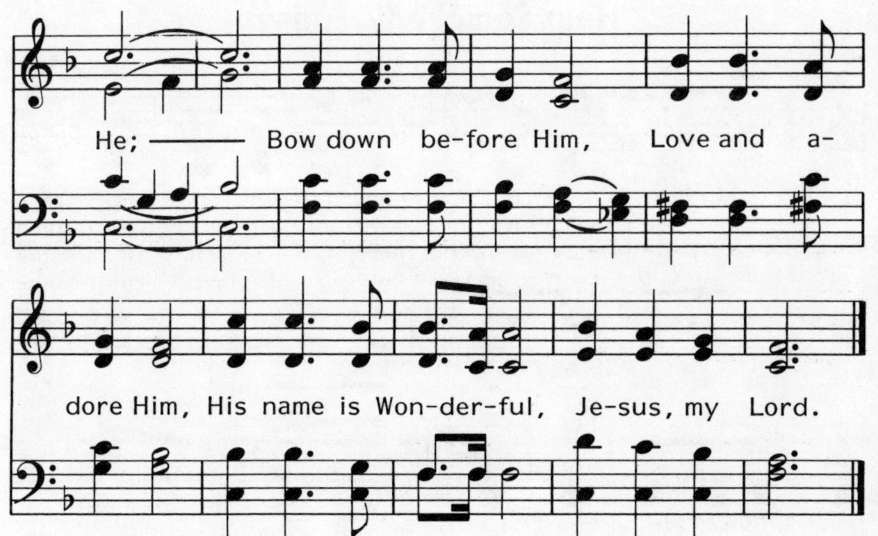
He; —— Bow down be-fore Him, Love and a-
dore Him, His name is Won-der-ful, Je-sus, my Lord.

Shalom Chaverim

Israeli Round

Dm
*
Sha - lom, cha-ve-rim! Sha - lom, cha-ve-rim!
Fare-well, good friends, Fare - well, good friends,
Bb C7 F Dm
Sha - lo - - - om! Le - hit - ra - ot,
Fare - well, fare - well! Till we meet a - gain,
Bb Gm A7 Dm
le - hit - ra - ot, Sha - lo - - - - om.
till we meet a - gain, Fare - well, fare - well.

Pronounced "Shah-lohm chah-vay-reem"; ch like German "noch".
*Succeeding voices enter. English by A. D. Z.

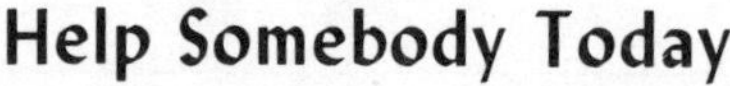
Help Somebody Today

Mrs. Frank A. Breck — Chas. H. Gabriel

1. Look all a-round you, find some-one in need, Help some-
2. Man - y are wait-ing a kind lov-ing word, Help some-
3. Man - y have bur-dens too heav - y to bear, Help some-
4. Some are dis-cour-aged and wear-y in heart, Help some-

bod-y to - day! — Tho' it be lit - tle, a
bod-y to - day! — Thou hast a mes-sage, O
bod-y to - day! — Grief is the por-tion of
bod-y to - day! — Some-one the jour-ney to

neigh-bor-ly deed, Help some-bod-y to - day —
let it be heard, Help some-bod-y to - day —
some ev - 'ry-where, Help some-bod-y to - day —
Heav-en should start, Help some-bod-y to - day —

CHORUS

Help some-bod-y to - day, — (to - day) Some-bod - y a-

long life's way —— Let sor-row be end-ed, The
home — ward way
friend-less be-friend-ed, Oh help some-bod-y to-day!
God Is Great
H.A. Cesar Malan
God is great and — God is good,
And we thank Him for our food.
By His hand may we be led, —
Give us Lord our dai —— ly – bread.
Give us Lord our – dai – ly bread.

In My Heart There Rings a Melody

Words and Music by Elton M. Roth

1. I have a song that Je-sus gave me, It was
sent from heaven a - bove;—There nev-er was a sweet-er
mel-o-dy, 'Tis a mel-o-dy of love.
CHORUS:
In my heart there rings a mel-o-dy, There rings a mel-o -

3
dy with heav-en's har-mo-ny; In my heart there
rings a mel-o-dy; There rings a mel-o-dy of love.

2. I love the Christ who died on Calvary,
For He washed my sins away;
He put within my heart a melody,
And I know it's there to stay.
(Chorus)

3. 'Twill be my endless theme in glory,
With the angels I will sing;
'Twill be a song with glorious harmony,
When the courts of heaven ring.
(Chorus)

Fellowship

2-Part Round
1
May — this our fel-low - ship for - tell
2
That we may learn in — peace to dwell.

Soon and Very Soon

A.C. Andrae Crouch

1.,4. Soon and ve - ry soon, — We are going to see the King; — Soon and ve-ry soon, — We are going to see the King; — Soon and ve-ry soon, — We are going to see the King; —
2. No more cry-ing there, — We are going to see the King; — No more cry-ing there, — We are going to see the King; — No more cry-ing there, — We are going to see the King; — Hal-le-
3. No more dy - ing there, — We are going to see the King; — No more dy-ing there, — We are going to see the King; — No more dy-ing there, — We are going to see the King; —

lu - jah! —— Hal-le - lu - jah! — We're going to

see the King. —— going to see the King. —

—— Hal— le - lu —— jah! Hal — le - lu —— jah!

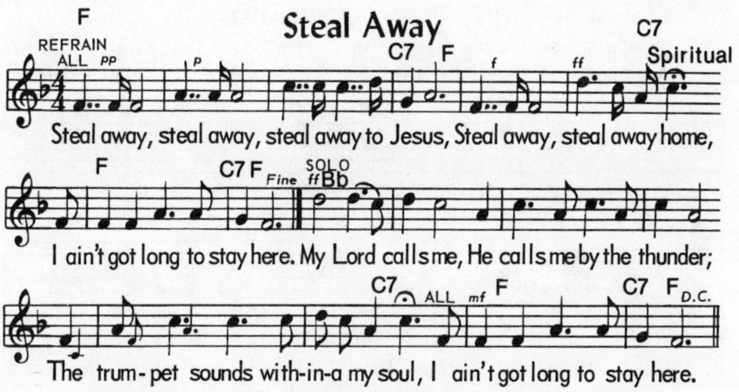
Steal Away
Spiritual
REFRAIN
ALL pp
F
p
C7 F
f
ff
C7
Steal away, steal away, steal away to Jesus, Steal away, steal away home,
F
C7 F Fine
SOLO
ff Bb
I ain't got long to stay here. My Lord calls me, He calls me by the thunder;
C7
ALL
mf F
C7 F D.C.
The trum-pet sounds with-in-a my soul, I ain't got long to stay here.

2. Green trees are bending, Poor sinner stands a-trembling;
3. Tombstones are bursting, Poor sinner stands a-trembling;
4. My Lord calls me, He calls me by the lightning;

America

Samuel F. Smith, 1832
English, c. 1740
G D7 G
1. My coun - try, 'tis of thee, Sweet land of
2. My na - tive coun - try thee, Land of the
3. Let mu - sic swell the breeze And ring thru
4. Our fa - thers' God, to Thee, Au - thor of
D7 G D7 G
lib - er - ty, Of thee I sing; Land where my
no - ble free, Thy name I love; I love thy
all the trees, Sweet free - dom's song; Let mor - tal
lib - er - ty, To Thee we sing; Long may our
D7
fa - thers died, Land of the Pil - grims' pride,
rocks and rills, Thy woods and tem - pled hills,
tongues a - wake, Let all that breathe par - take,
land be bright With free - dom's ho - ly light;
G C G D7 G
From ev - 'ry moun - tain - side Let free - dom ring.
My heart with rap - ture thrills Like that a - bove.
Let rocks their si - lence break, The sound pro - long.
Pro - tect us by Thy might, Great God, our King.

America the Beautiful

Katharine Lee Bates
Samuel A. Ward
O beau-ti-ful for spacious skies, For am-ber waves of grain,
O beau-ti-ful for pil-grim feet, Whose stern, im-passion'd stress
O beau-ti-ful for he-roes proved In lib-er-a-ting strife,
O beau-ti-ful for pa-triot dream That sees be-yond the years
For pur-ple mountain maj-es-ties A-bove the fruit-ed plain.
A thor-ough-fare for freedom beat A-cross the wil-der-ness.
Who more than self their Country loved, And mer-cy more than life.
Thine al-a-bas-ter cit-ies gleam Undim'd by hu-man tears.
A-mer-i-ca! A-mer-i-ca! God shed His grace on thee, And
A-mer-i-ca! A-mer-i-ca! God mend thine ev-'ry flaw, Con-
A-mer-i-ca! A-mer-i-ca! May God thy gold re-fine, Till
A-mer-i-ca! A-mer-i-ca! God shed His grace on thee, And
crown thy good with broth-er-hood From sea to shin-ing sea!
firm thy soul in self-con-trol, Thy lib-er-ty in law.
all suc-cess be no-ble-ness, And ev-'ry gain di-vine.
crown thy good with broth-er-hood From sea to shin-ing sea!

This Land Is Your Land

W.G. Woody Guthrie

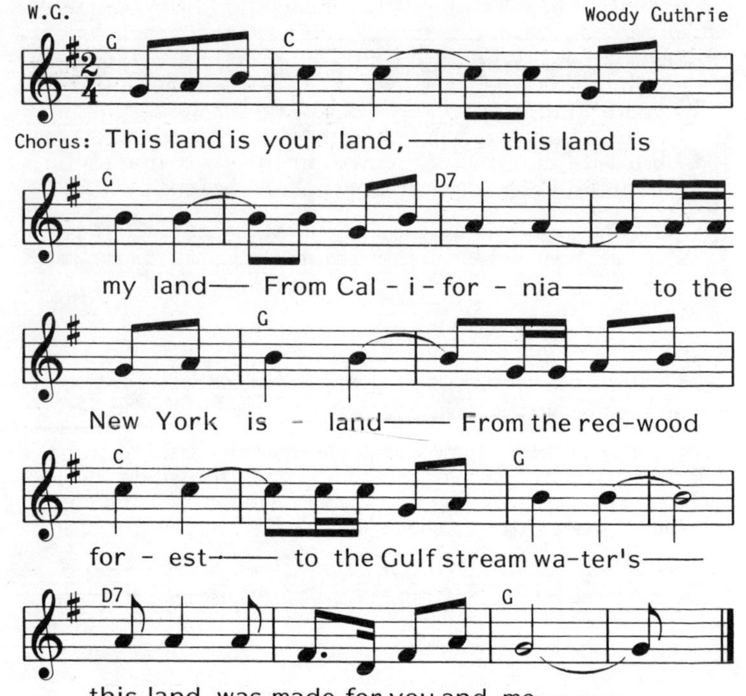
G
C
Chorus: This land is your land, — this land is
G
D7
my land — From Cal - i - for - nia — to the
G
New York is - land — From the red-wood
C
G
for - est — to the Gulf stream wa-ter's —
D7
G
this land was made for you and me. —

1. As I went walking that ribbon of highway,
   I saw above me that endless skyway,
   I saw below me that golden valley,
   This land was made for you and me. (Chorus)

2. When the sun come shining, then I was strolling,
   And the wheat fields waving, and the dust clouds rolling.
   A voice was chanting as the fog was lifting,
   This land was made for you and me.

3. In the squares of the city by the shadow of the steeple,
   Near the relief office, I saw my people.
   And some were stumbling, and some were wond'ring if
   This land was made for you and me.

Song of Peace
FINLANDIA
Lloyd Stone
Jean Sibelius
1. This is my song, O God of all the na-tions, A
2. My coun-try's skies are blu - er than the o - cean, And
song of peace for lands a - far and mine; This is my
sun-light beams on clo-ver-leaf and pine. But oth - er
home, the coun-try where my heart is, Here are my hopes, my
lands have sun-light, too, and clo - ver, And skies are ev - 'ry-
dreams, my ho - ly shrine; But oth-er hearts in oth-er lands are
where as blue as mine. O hear my song, thou God of all the
beat-ing With hopes and dreams as true and high as mine.
na - tions, A song of peace for their land and for mine.
Words © 1934 by Lorenz Publishing Co. Tune by permission of Breitkopf & Hartel.

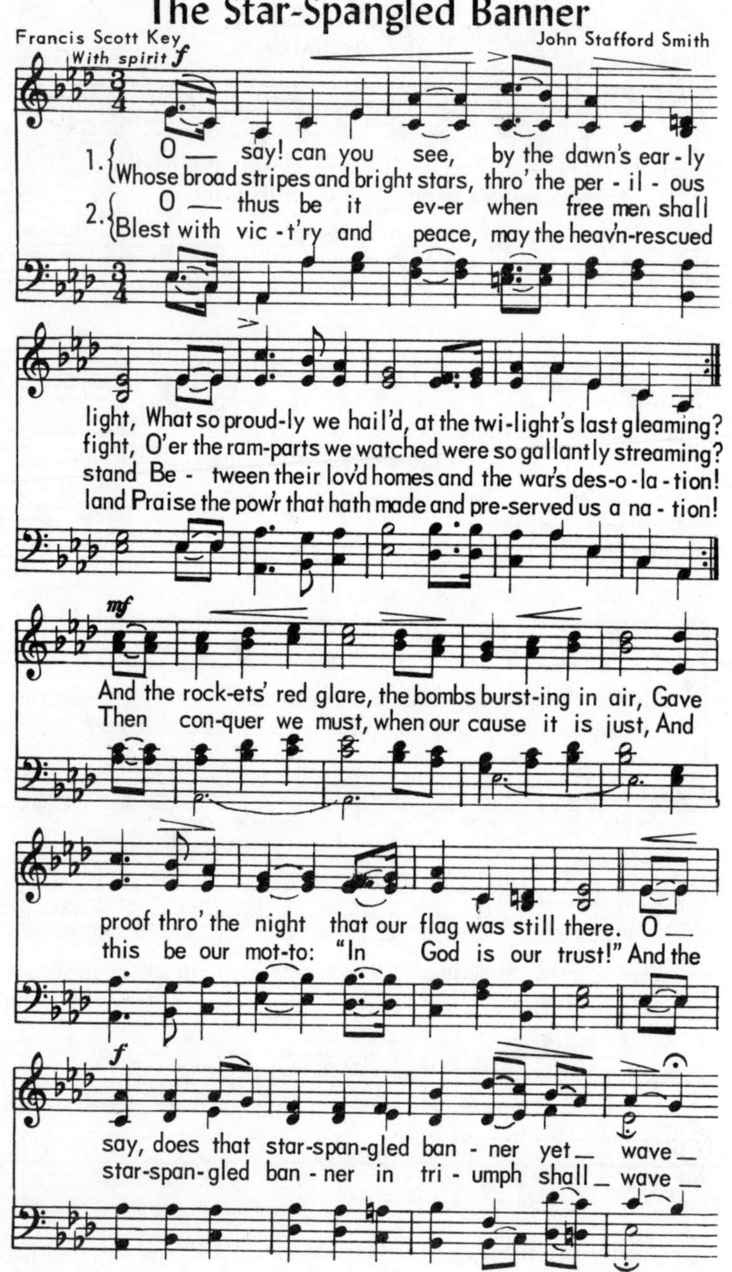
The Star-Spangled Banner
Francis Scott Key
John Stafford Smith
With spirit
1. O — say! can you see, by the dawn's ear - ly light, What so proud-ly we hail'd, at the twi-light's last gleaming?
Whose broad stripes and bright stars, thro' the per - il - ous fight, O'er the ram-parts we watched were so gallantly streaming?
2. O — thus be it ev-er when free men shall stand Be - tween their lov'd homes and the war's des-o - la - tion!
Blest with vic - t'ry and peace, may the heav'n-rescued land Praise the pow'r that hath made and pre-served us a na - tion!
And the rock-ets' red glare, the bombs burst-ing in air, Gave proof thro' the night that our flag was still there. O — say, does that star-span-gled ban - ner yet — wave —
Then con-quer we must, when our cause it is just, And this be our mot-to: "In God is our trust!" And the star-span-gled ban - ner in tri - umph shall — wave —

ff
O'er the land of the free and the home of the brave?
brave!

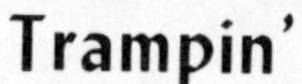

Trampin'

Spiritual

Leader Eb All

I'm a-tramp - in', tramp - in', Tryin' to make

Bb Eb Leader

heav-en my home, Hal - le - lu - jah! I'm a-

All F Bb

tramp-in', tramp-in', Tryin' to make heav-en my

Eb *Fine* Leader

home. 1. I've nev-er been to heav-en, but

All F Bb

I've— been told, Tryin' to make heav-en my

Eb Leader

home, That the streets up there are paved—with

All F Bb Eb *D. C.*

gold; Tryin' to make heav-en my home.

Let There Be Peace on Earth

S.M. & J.J. Sy Miller & Jill Jackson

C Am Dm7 G7 C F
Let there be peace on earth And let it be-
C Dm G7 C B7
gin with me —— Let there be peace on
Em B7 G9 G7
earth, The peace that was meant to be. ——
Am Em C7 F
With God as our ma-ker, —— All one
G7 C Am7 D7
fa - mi - ly. —— Let me walk with my
G Am7 D7 G7
neigh-bor —— In per- fect har - mo - ny.
C Am Dm7 G7
—— Let peace be - gin with me, Let
C F C Dm G7 C
this be the mo - ment now —— With
B7 Em
ev - 'ry step I take, Let this be my

B7
G9
G7
C
sol - emn vow: ——— To take each
C+
F
mo-ment and live each mo-ment in peace e-
Bdim Am
D7
Fm6
C
E7
ter - na - ly. ——— Let there be
F
C
C7
1F Dm7
G7
C
peace on earth And let it be-gin with me.
G7
2 F E7 Am
Dm7 G7
Dm7
C
let it be - gin with me. ———

Day Is Done

TAPS

Day is done, Gone the sun, From the lake, From the hills,
Thanks and praise For our days 'Neath the sun, 'Neath the stars,
From the sky; All is well, Safe-ly rest, God is nigh.
'Neath the sky; As we go, This we know, God is nigh.

Were You There?

Spiritual

1. Were you there when they cru-ci-fied my Lord? Were you
2. Were you there when they nailed Him to the tree? Were you
3. Were you there when they laid Him in the tomb? Were you
there when they cru-ci-fied my Lord?
there when they nailed Him to the tree? Oh!
there when they laid Him in the tomb?
Some-times it caus-es me to trem-ble, trem-ble, trem-ble,
Were you there — when they cru - ci - fied my Lord?
Were you there — when they nailed Him to the tree?
Were you there — when they laid Him in the tomb?

2. Were you there on that glorious Easter morn?
Were you there on that glorious Easter morn?
O, sometimes it makes me feel like shoutin',
shoutin', shoutin',
Were you there on that glorious Easter morn?

Do Lord

Spiritual

G
CHORUS: Do Lord, oh do Lord, oh do re-mem-ber
C
me. Do Lord, oh do Lord, oh
G
do re-mem-ber me. Do Lord, oh
B7
Em
Do Lord, oh do re-mem-ber me. Look a-
G
D7
G
way be - yond — the blue.

1. I've got a home in glory land that outshines the sun. (3x)
   Look away beyond the blue.
2. I've got a heavenly Father who's waiting there for me. (3x)
   Look away beyond the blue.

Note: This song is often jazzed up, but this version is intended to be sung at a moderate tempo.

Balm in Gilead
Lento
REFRAIN
Spiritual
pp
There is a balm in Gil - e - ad To make the
wound-ed whole, There is a balm in Gil - e - ad To
p rit. Fine
SOLO
mf cresc.
heal the sin-sick soul.
1. Some - times I feel dis -
2. If you don't preach like
p Hm
Hm
cour-aged, And think my work's in vain. But then the Ho-ly
Pe - ter, If you don't pray like Paul, Just tell the love of
Hm
Hm
Tutti
mf
pp
Spir-it Re - vives my soul a - gain.
Je - sus And say He died for all.
There is a

From "Twelve Negro Spirituals" Arranged by Daniel L. Ridout. By permission.

I Want Jesus to Walk With Me

Spiritual

Unison
1. I want Je-sus to walk with me;
2. In my tri-als, Lord, walk with me;
3. When I'm in trou-ble, Lord, walk with me;
I want Je-sus to walk with me;
In my tri-als, Lord, walk with me;
When I'm in trou-ble, Lord, walk with me;
All a-long my pil-grim jour-ney,
When my heart is al-most break-ing,
When my head is bowed in sor-row,
Lord, I want Je-sus to walk with me.

Lord's Prayer Chant
Tune set down by Olive Pattison
West Indian Folk Tune
Our Fa-ther, which art in hea-ven,
A REFRAIN
cresc.
Hal-low-ed-a-be thy Name.
Thy king-dom come, Thy will be done,
B REFRAIN
Hal-low-ed-a-be thy Name.
to A
On the earth as it is in hea-ven.
(Sing B REFRAIN)
Give us this day our dai-ly bread,
to A
And for-give us all our tres-pas-ses,
to B
As we for-give those who tres-pass a-gainst us,
to A
And leave us not to the dev-il to be temp-ted,
to B
But de-liv-er us from all that is e-vil,
cresc.
to A
For thine is the king-dom, The pow-er and the glo-ry,

mf
to B
For ev - er, for ev - er, for ev-er and ev - er,
to A
A - men, A - men, A - men, A - men,
A - men, A - men, A - men, A - men.
rall.
molto rit.
Hal-low-ed-a-be thy name.

Repeat A .... * or B .... * as indicated after alternate lines.

King of Kings

Arr. by Olive J. Williams
Spiritual

Joyfully

Refrain

A7 D A D A D A D

He is King of Kings. He is Lord of Lords.

Bm A D G6 D A D *Fine*

Je-sus Christ the first and last, — No man works like Him.

D A D G6 D A D

1. I know that my Re-deem-er lives, No man works like Him.
2. O sin-ner if you will be-lieve,

D A D G6 D A D D.C.

And by His love sweet blessing gives, No man works like Him.
Grace of the Lord you will re-ceive,

Swing Low, Sweet Chariot

Spiritual
mp Solo F C7 mf F Chorus C7
Swing low, sweet char-i - ot, Com-in' for to car-ry me home!
Solo F C7 Chorus F C7 Fine. F
Swing low, sweet char-i - ot, Com-in' for to car-ry me home.
Solo f F C7
I looked ov-er Jor-dan, an' what did I see,
ff Chorus F C7 mf Solo F
Com-in' for to car-ry me home! A band of an-gels
C7 mp Chorus F C7 F D.C.
Com-in' af-ter me, Com-in' for to car-ry me home.

2. If you get there before I do,
   Jes' tell my fren's that I'm a-comin' too, . . .
3. I'm sometimes up an' sometimes down,
   But still my soul feels heavenly boun', . . .

(Companion song to "All Night, All Day")

Standing in the Need of Prayer

Spirtual
Chorus G Humbly It's me D7 G
It's-a me, it's-a me, O, Lord, standing in the
D7 G 1 2 Leader G
need of prayer. prayer. 1. Not my broth-er, not my sis-ter, but-a
Chorus D7 G 1 2
me, O, Lord, stand-ing in the need of prayer. prayer.

2. Not my father, not my mother, . . .
3. Not my preacher, not my teacher, . . .

Note: The chorus may hum last chord of chorus while leader sings.

All Night, All Day

Spiritual

F Bb
All night, all day, an-gels watch-in' o-ver me, my

F C7 F Fine
Lord.__ All night, all day, an-gels watch-in' o-ver me.__

F Bb
1. Now I lay me down__ to sleep An-gels
2. If I die be-fore__ I wake An-gels

F
watch-in' o-ver me, my Lord__ Pray the Lord my
watch-in' o-ver me, my Lord__ Pray the Lord my

C7 F
soul__ to keep An-gels watch-in' o-ver me.
soul__ to take An-gels watch-in' o-ver me.
D. C. al Fine

3. If I live another day
Pray the Lord to guide my way.

Companion song to "Swing Low, Sweet Chariot"

I'm Gonna Sing

G
1. I'm gon-na sing when the Spir-it says "Sing,"__ I'm gon-na
G D7
sing when the Spir-it says "Sing,"__ I'm gon-na sing when the
C G D7
Spir-it says "Sing,"__ And o-bey the Spir-it of the Lord.__
2. Shout. . . 3. Preach. . . 4. Pray. . . 5. Sing. . .

Come and Go

Spiritual — Collected by Olive J. Williams

Solo
Group
F
B♭
G7
C
C7
Dm
F7
1. Come an' go to that lan', Come an' go to that
2. There is joy in that lan', There is joy in that
lan', Come an' go to that lan' Where I'm boun', where I'm
lan', There is joy in that lan' Where I'm boun', where I'm
boun'. Come an' go to that lan', Come an' go to that
boun'. There is joy in that lan', There is joy in that
lan', Come an' go to that lan' where I'm boun'.
lan', There is joy in that lan' where I'm boun'.

3. Peace an' happiness in that lan', . . .
4. There'll be singing in the lan', voices ringing in that land.
5. There'll be freedom in that lan', . . .
6. Come an' go to that lan', . . .

Kum Ba Yah

(Come By Here)

Slowly
Spiritual
C
F
Dm
G
G7
Kum ba yah, my Lord, Kum ba yah! Kum ba
yah, my Lord, Kum ba yah! Kum ba yah, my Lord,
Kum ba yah! Oh, Lord, Kum ba yah!

2. Someone's crying, Lord, Kum ba yah!
3. Someone's singing, Lord, Kum ba yah!
4. Someone's praying, Lord, Kum ba yah!

Rise and Shine
Anonymous
Traditional
C F
Rise and shine and give God the glo-ry, glo-ry,
C Dm7 F/G C
Rise and shine and give God the glo-ry, glo-ry, Rise and
Dm7 F C G C
Fine
shine and give God the glo-ry, glo-ry; Chil-dren of the Lord.—
Lord, I Want to Be a Christian
Key to: D
Spiritual
Solo D All
1. Lord I want to be a Christ-ian In-a my heart,
A7 Bm
in-a my heart,—Lord, I want to be a Christ-ian
G D G D Bm
in-a my heart, — In-a my heart, — In-a my heart,—

D A7 Bm G D

Lord, I want to be a Christ-ian In-a my heart.—

2. ..more loving– 3. ..more holy– 4. ..like Jesus–

From *Dett's Religious Folk Songs of the Negro.* By permission.

I'm Gonna Sing, Sing, Sing

Traditional
G
I'm gon - na sing, sing, sing, I'm gon - na shout, shout, shout,
D7
I'm gon - na sing, I'm gon-na shout, praise the Lord, And when those
G C G
gates are o - pen wide, I'm gon-na be on Je - sus' side,
D7 G
I'm gon - na sing, I'm gon - na shout, praise the Lord.

Jacob's Ladder

Spiritual
D
We are climb-ing Ja - cob's lad-der,
A A7 G D
We are climb-ing Ja-cob's lad - der,
Bm G D
We are climb-ing Ja - cob's lad - der,
Sol-diers of the cross.
(Bro - thers, sis - ters, all.)

2. Ev'ry rung goes higher, higher...
3. Sinner, do you love my Jesus?...
4. If you love Him, why not serve Him?...
5. We are climbing higher, higher...

Go Down, Moses

With dramatic intensity Arr. by Olive J. Williams

LEADER
CHORUS
Broadly
When Is-rael was in E-gypt's land:
Thus saith the Lord, bold Mo-ses said: Let my peo-ple
O let us all from bond-age flee,
LEADER
CHORUS
Op-press'd so hard they could not stand,
go; If not I'll smite your first-born dead, Let my people
And let us all in Christ be free!
REFRAIN
go. Go down, Mo-ses, 'way down in E-gypt's land,
LEADER
CHORUS
Tell ol' Pha-raoh Let my peo-ple go.

Let Us Break Bread Together
Spiritual
1. Let us break bread to - geth - er on our knees.
2. Let us drink wine to - geth - er on our knees.
3. Let us praise God to - geth - er on our knees.
Let us break bread to - geth - er on our knees.
Let us drink wine to - geth - er on our knees.
Let us praise God to - geth - er on our knees.
When I fall down on my knees with my face to the ris - ing
sun, Oh, Lord have mer - cy on me.

Amen
Key to: D
Arr. by Marion Downs
Spiritual
Chorus
D
A7
A - men, A - men, A - men, A-
Solo Obbligato
1. See the ba - by,
2. See Him in the tem - ple,
3. See Him at the sea - side,
4. See Him in the gar - den,
5. Yes, He is my Sav - ior,
D A7 D
1 Chorus
2
men, A - men. men, A - men.
A -
Ly-ing in a man-ger One Christ-mas morn-ing.
Talk-ing to the El-ders, How they marvelled at His wis-dom.
Preach-ing and heal - ing, To the blind and the fee-ble.
Pray - ing to His Fa - ther, In deep - est sor - row.
Je - sus died to save us, And He rose on Eas - ter.
men, A - men, A -
6. Hal - le-lu - jah In the King-
men, A-men, A-men. A - men,
dom with my Sav - ior. A - men, A-men,
A - men, A - men, A-men, A-men.

Amen— pronounce A as in bay.

We Shall Overcome

American Freedom Song

Slowly
B♭ E♭ B♭ E♭
1. We shall o - ver - come, We shall o - ver-
B♭ E♭ F7 Gm C7
come, We shall o - ver - come some
F C7 F F7 B♭ E♭ B♭
day; Oh! Deep in my heart
E♭ F7 Gm B♭ E♭ B♭ F7 B♭
I do be-lieve, We shall o - ver -come some day.

2. We'll walk hand in hand.....
3. Truth shall make us free.....
4. Black and white together.....
5. The Lord will see us through.....
6. We shall live in peace.....
7. Whole wide world around.....

New words and musical arrangement by Zilphia Horton, Frank Hamilton. Guy Carawan and Pete Seeger.

Happy Days

Round

1
Hap-py days to all those that we love! Hap-py
2
days to all those that love us! Hap-py days to all those that love
3
them that love those that love them that love those that love us.

The Old Time Religion

F7
Bb

CHO. 'Tis the old time re-lig-ion, 'Tis the
1. It was good for Paul and Si - las, It was
2. Makes me love ev - 'ry-bod-y, Makes me
3. It will take us all to hea-ven, It will

F7
Bb
Bb
+7

old time re-lig-ion, 'Tis the old time re-
good for Paul and Si - las, It was good for Paul and
love ev - ry-bod-y, Makes me love ev-'ry-
take us all to hea-ven, It will take us all to

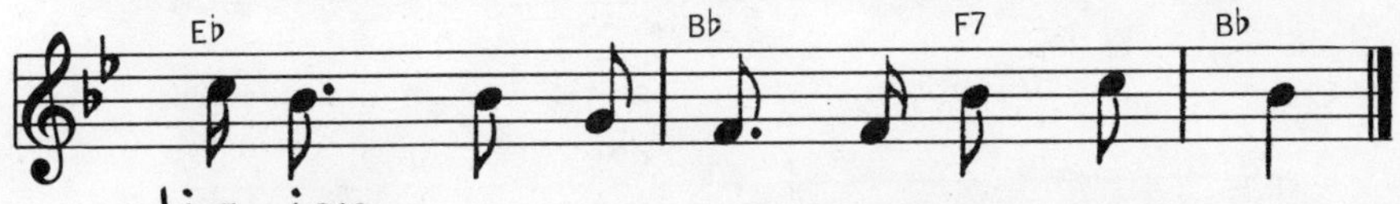
Eb
Bb
F7
Bb

lig - ion,
Si - las,
bod - y,
hea - ven,
And it's good e-nough for me.

For Thy Gracious Blessings

4-Part Canon

1
2
3
For Thy gra-cious bless - ings, For Thy
4
won-drous Word; For Thy lov - ing
kind —— ness, We give thanks, O God.

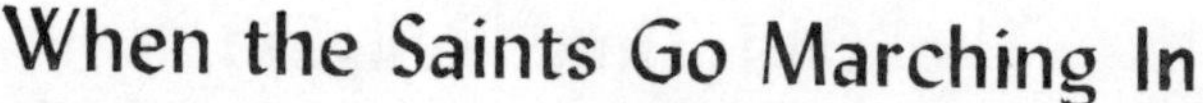

When the Saints Go Marching In

Spiritual

1. Oh, when the saints Oh, when the saints go march-ing
2. Up where the streets Up where the streets are paved with

in, go march-ing in, Oh, when the saints go march-ing
gold, are paved with gold Up where the streets are paved with

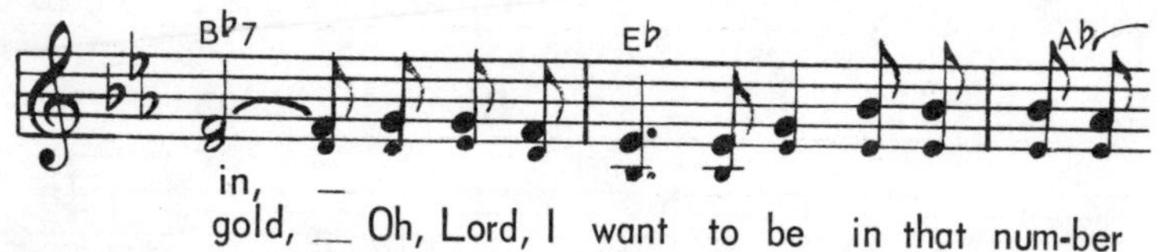

in, —
gold, — Oh, Lord, I want to be in that num-ber

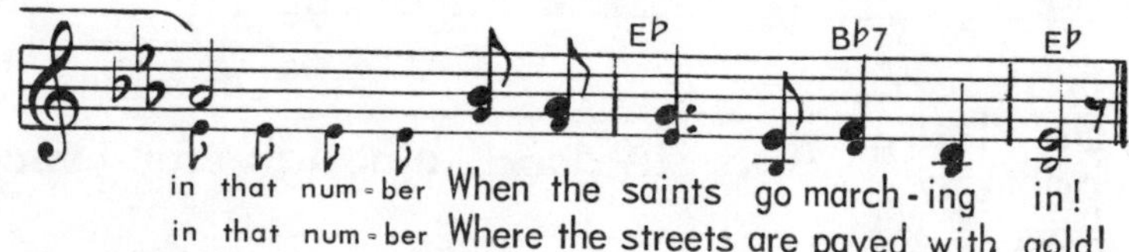

in that num-ber When the saints go march-ing in!
in that num-ber Where the streets are paved with gold!

3. Oh, when the stars refuse to shine......

Rocka My Soul

Spiritual

Rock-a my soul — in the bo-som of A - bra-ham;
Rock-a my soul — in the bo-som of A - bra-ham;
Rock-a my soul — in the bo-som of A - bra ham;

C F Fine F
Oh, rock-a my soul. So high, you can't get o-ver it;
C7 F
So low, you can't get un-der it; So wide, you
C F D.C.
can't get a-round_it; You must go in at the door.

Can be sung with "He's Got the Whole World"

Ev'ry Time I Feel the Spirit

arr. by Marion Downs

Spiritual

Chorus

Ev-'ry time I ___ feel the Spir-it ___ Mov-in'
in my heart, _ I will pray, _ Ev-'ry time I __ feel the
Spir-it ___ Mov-in' in my heart, __ I will pray. __ Fine

Hum

1. Up-on the moun-tain, when my Lord spoke, _ Out of God's
2. Oh, I have sor-rows, and I have woe __ And I have

mouth came _ fire and smoke; _ Look'd all a-round _ me
heart-ache _ here be-low; _ But while God leads _ me

it look'd so fine __ Till I ask'd my Lord _ if all were mine.
I'll nev-er fear For I am shel-tered by God's care. D.C.

NOTE: Low voices sing melody; high voices hum obligato

Good News

REFRAIN
Lively and bright
mf
Spiritual
Good news! The char-i-ot's com-ing. Good news! The
char-i-ot's com-ing. Good news! The char-i-ot's com-ing,
Fine
There's a
And I don't want it to leave me be-hind. 1. There's a
long white robe in the heav-en I know
cresc.
long white robe in the heav-en I know
A long white
A long white
p
robe in the heav-en I know. There's a long white robe in the
robe in the heav-en I know.
D.C.
heav-en I know, And I don't want it to leave me be-hind.
2. pair of wings.. 3. shoes... 4. starry crown... 5. golden harp..

Go Tell It on the Mountain

Jubilantly
Spiritual
Go tell it on the moun - tain,
Tell it on the moun - tain
D G G
O - ver the hills and ev - 'ry - where, Go tell it on the
G D7 Fine
moun - tain that Je - sus Christ is - a - born.
Tell it on the moun - tain
G D G
1. When I was a sin - ner, I prayed both night and day: I
2. When I was a seek - er, I sought both night and day; I
3. God made me a watch - man up - on the cit - y wall; And
G A7 D.C.
asked the Lord to help me, and God showed me the way.
asked my Lord to help me, and God taught me to pray.
if I am a Chris - tian, I am the least of all.

While by My Sheep

JÜNGST Irregular

From the German

Seventeenth Century Carol
Arr. by Hugo Jungst (1853-1923); Alt.

f
p echo
1. While by my sheep I watched at night, Glad ti-dings
2. There shall be born, so he did say, In Beth-le-
3. There shall the Child lie in a stall, This Child who
4. This gift of God we'll cher-ish well, That ev-er
brought an an-gel bright. How great my joy! Great my joy!
hem a Child to-day; How great my joy! Great my joy!
shall re-deem us all. How great our joy! Great our joy!
joy our hearts shall fill. How great our joy! Great our joy!
Joy, joy, joy! Joy, joy, joy! Praise we the Lord in
Joy, joy, joy! Joy, joy, joy! Praise we the Lord in
Joy, joy, joy! Joy, joy, joy! Praise we the Lord in
Joy, joy, joy! Joy, joy, joy! Praise we the Lord in
heaven on high! Praise we the Lord in heaven on high!
heaven on high! Praise we the Lord in heaven on high!
heaven on high! Praise we the Lord in heaven on high!
heaven on high! Praise we the Lord in heaven on high!

Silent Night

Joseph Mohr | Franz Gruber

C
G7
1. Si - lent night, ho - ly night, All is calm,
2. Si - lent night, ho - ly night, Dark-ness flies,
3. Si - lent night, ho - ly night, Son of God,
4. Si - lent night, ho - ly night, Won-drous star,
C
F
C
all is bright; Round yon Vir - gin Mother and Child!
all is light; Shepherds hear the an - gels sing,
love's pure light; Ra - diant beams from Thy ho - ly face,
lend thy light; With the an - gels let __ us sing,
F
C
G7
Ho - ly In - fant, so ten - der and mild, Sleep in heav - en - ly
"Al - le - lu - ia! hail the King! Christ the Sav - iour is
With the dawn of re - deem - ing grace, Je - sus, Lord, at Thy
Al - le - lu - ia to __ our King; Christ the Sav - iour is
C
G7
C
peace, __ Sleep in heav - en - ly peace. __
born, __ Christ the Sav - iour is born." __
birth, __ Je - sus, Lord, at Thy birth. __
born, __ Christ the Sav - iour is born. __

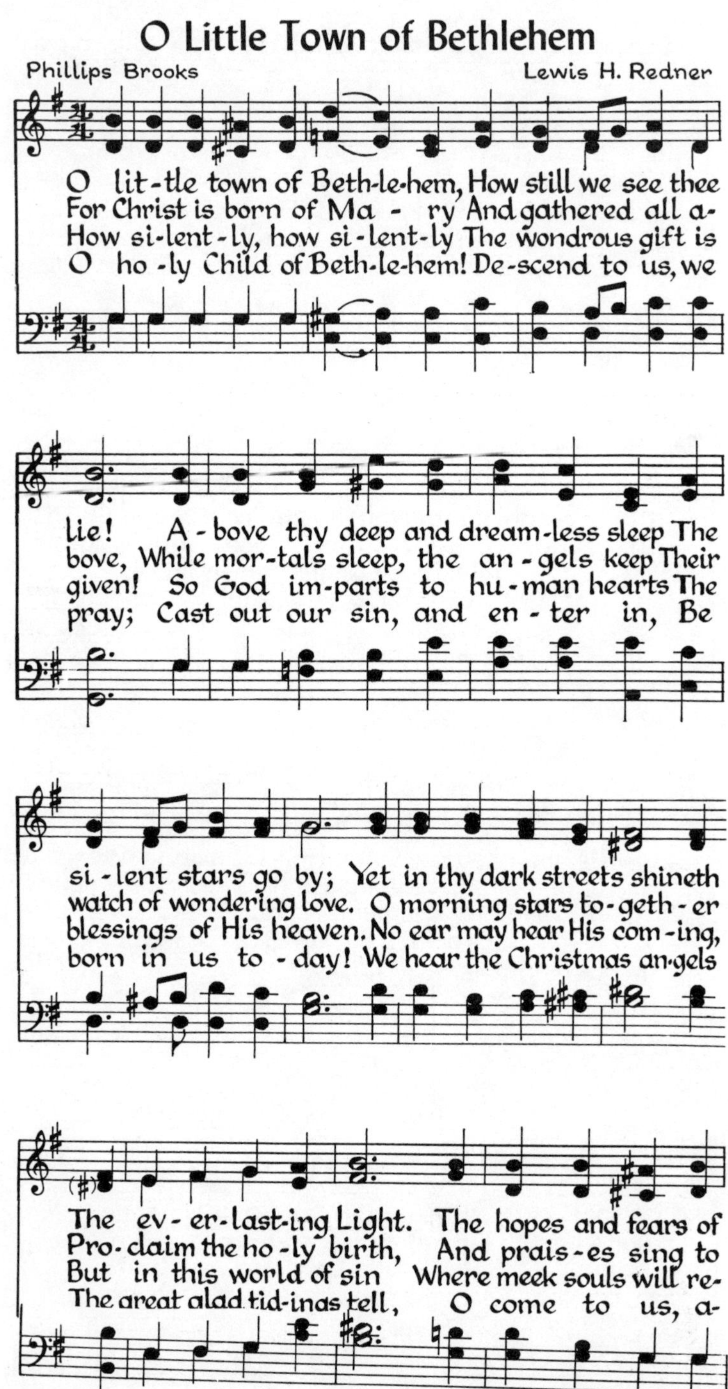
O Little Town of Bethlehem
Phillips Brooks
Lewis H. Redner
O lit-tle town of Beth-le-hem, How still we see thee
For Christ is born of Ma - ry And gathered all a-
How si-lent-ly, how si-lent-ly The wondrous gift is
O ho-ly Child of Beth-le-hem! De-scend to us, we
lie! A-bove thy deep and dream-less sleep The
bove, While mor-tals sleep, the an-gels keep Their
given! So God im-parts to hu-man hearts The
pray; Cast out our sin, and en-ter in, Be
si-lent stars go by; Yet in thy dark streets shineth
watch of wondering love. O morning stars to-geth-er
blessings of His heaven. No ear may hear His com-ing,
born in us to-day! We hear the Christmas an-gels
The ev-er-last-ing Light. The hopes and fears of
Pro-claim the ho-ly birth, And prais-es sing to
But in this world of sin Where meek souls will re-
The great glad tid-ings tell, O come to us, a-

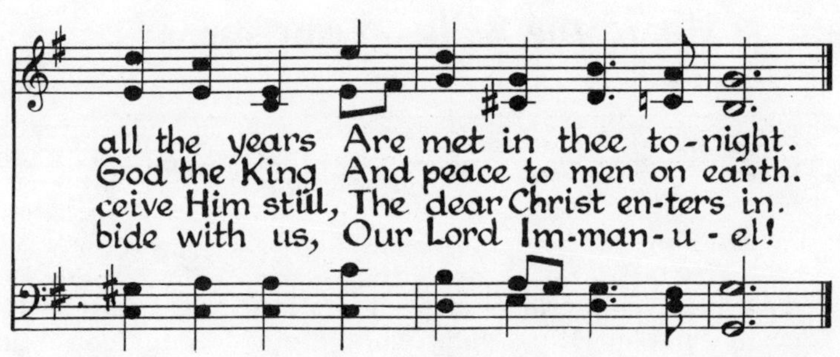
all the years Are met in thee to-night.
God the King And peace to men on earth.
ceive Him still, The dear Christ en-ters in.
bide with us, Our Lord Im-man-u-el!

Up on the Housetop

B.H. B. Hanby

1. Up on the house-top — rein-deer pause,
Out jumps good old San-ta Claus; Down thru the
chim-ney with lots of toys, all for the
lit-tle one's Christ-mas joys.

CHORUS

Ho, ho, ho!
Who would-n't go? Ho, ho, ho! Who would-n't
go? — Up on the house-top click, click, click,
Down thru the chim-ney with good Saint Nick.

I Heard the Bells on Christmas Day

Henry W. Longfellow — Jean Baptiste Calkin

1. I heard the bells on Christ-mas day Their
2. I thought how, as the day had come, The
3. And in de-spair I bowed my head: "There
4. Yet pealed the bells more loud and deep: "God
5. Then ring - ing sing - ing on it's way, The
old fa - mil - iar car-ols play, And wild and sweet the
bel-fries of all Christ-en-dom Had rolled a-long th'un-
is no peace on earth," I said, "For hate is strong, and
is not dead, nor doth he sleep; The wrong shall fail, the
world re-volved from night to day. A voice a chime, a
words re-peat Of
bro-ken song Of
mocks the song Of
right pre-vail With
chant sub-blime Of
peace on earth, good will to men.

O Come, All Ye Faithful

ADESTE FIDELES

Latin Hymn, 18th Century
Tr. Frederick Oakeley, 1841

Wade's *Cantus Diversi, 1751*

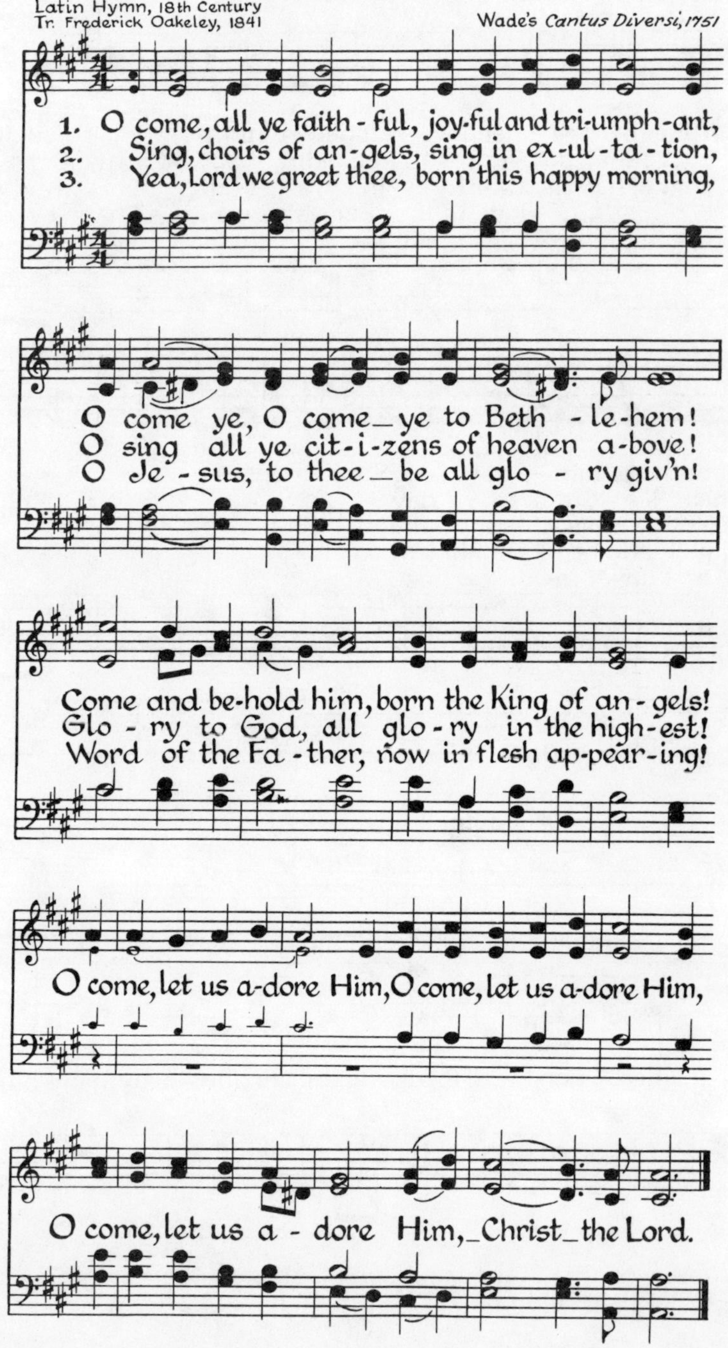
1. O come, all ye faith - ful, joy-ful and tri-umph-ant,
2. Sing, choirs of an-gels, sing in ex-ul-ta-tion,
3. Yea, Lord we greet thee, born this happy morning,
O come ye, O come_ye to Beth - le-hem!
O sing all ye cit-i-zens of heaven a-bove!
O Je - sus, to thee_be all glo - ry giv'n!
Come and be-hold him, born the King of an-gels!
Glo - ry to God, all glo-ry in the high-est!
Word of the Fa-ther, now in flesh ap-pear-ing!
O come, let us a-dore Him, O come, let us a-dore Him,
O come, let us a - dore Him,_Christ_the Lord.

How Great Our Joy

Traditional German Carol

arr. Hugo Jüngst

1. While by the sheep we watched at night, Glad ti-dings brought an an - gel bright.
2. There shall be born, so he did say, In Beth-le hem a Child to - day.
3. There shall the Child lie in a stall, This Child who shall re-deem us all.
4. This gift of God we'll cher-ish well, That ev-er joy our hearts shall fill.
How great our joy! Great our joy! Joy, joy, joy! Joy, joy, joy! Praise we the Lord in- heav'n on high! Praise we the Lord in- heav'n on high!
f
p
echo

Joy to the World

ANTIOCH

Isaac Watts George F. Handel

Joy to the world! the Lord is come: Let earth re-
Joy to the earth! the Sav-iour reigns: Let men their
He rules the world with truth and grace, And makes the
ceive her King; Let ev - ery heart pre-pare Him room,
songs em-ploy; While fields and floods, rocks, hills, and plains
na - tions prove The glo - ries of His right-eous-ness,
And heaven and na-ture sing, And heaven and na-
Re - peat the sound-ing joy, Re - peat the sound-
And won - ders of His love, And won-ders of
And heaven and na-ture sing,
Re - peat the sound-ing joy,
And won-ders of His love,
ture sing, And heaven, and heaven and na-ture sing.
ing joy, Re - peat, re-peat the sound-ing joy.
His love, And won-ders, won-ders of His love.
And heaven and na-ture sing.
Re - peat the sound-ing joy.
And won - ders of His love.

180

Stars of Ice
T'ien Ching-Fu
Trans. by Bliss Wiant
Chinese Carol
Fan T'ien-hsiang (Bliss Wiant)
Yi lun ming yueh, shu tien han hsing Ying chao yang shen se ju yin Shu wei mu jen ho ai ho ch'-in Wei tso ts'ao ti hsu han wen. Chi kuang ts'an lan ke sheng sse mang Mu jen fu fu e ch'ieh ching yun chung t'ien shih
Stars of ice, wheel of moon-light bright, Shine on sheep with sil-v'ry light; Hum-ble shep-herds chat-ting cir-cled round, Sit con-tent on gras-sy heights; Sud-den light! Hark, the an-gels sing! Shep-herds crouch in awe. Mid the clouds the
Dies the song, stars and moon gent-ly fade, Shep-herds leap for ver-y joy; Leave their qui-et flocks home-ward quick-ly fly, Wor-ship then the Ho-ly Boy, Won-drous news thru the streets re-sounds, Glad prais-es fill ev'ry home. Poor man's Sav-iour,
Learn-ed men from far east-ern lands Kneel be-fore the Ho-ly Child, Bring a-bun-dant gifts, rare, lux-u-ri-ant, Crowd the age-worn vil-lage inn. Miles on miles had they come to a-dore; No dis-tance seemed too far. Bound-less, sav-ing,

pao kao t'ung sheng Shen tzu yi sheng Po - li - hung
an-gels pro-claim: God's Son is born in Beth - le-hem.
peas - ant's Friend, Comes to - day to Beth - le-hem.
peace - ful love Now has come to Beth - le-hem.

Jingle, Bells

J. P. J. Pierpont

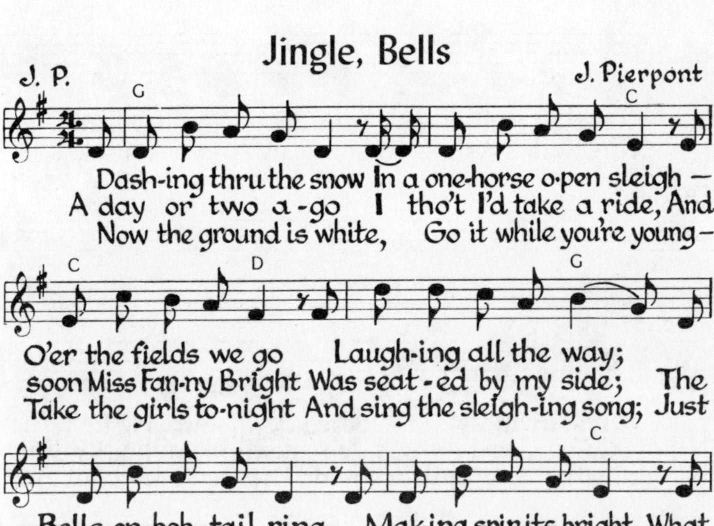
Dash-ing thru the snow In a one-horse o-pen sleigh —
A day or two a - go I tho't I'd take a ride, And
Now the ground is white, Go it while you're young -
O'er the fields we go Laugh-ing all the way;
soon Miss Fan-ny Bright Was seat - ed by my side; The
Take the girls to-night And sing the sleigh-ing song; Just

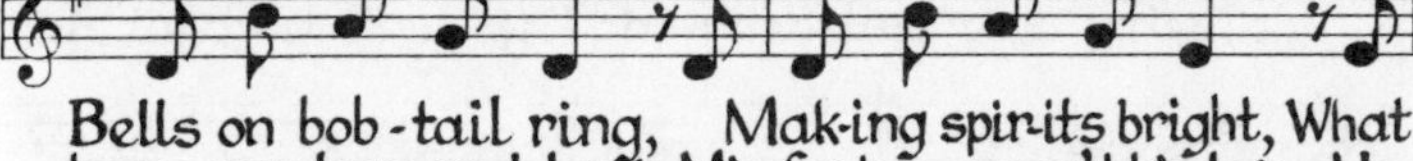
Bells on bob - tail ring, Mak-ing spir-its bright, What
horse was lean and lank, Mis-for-tune seem'd his lot, He
get a bob-tailed nag, Two-for - ty for his speed, Then

fun it is to ride and sing A sleigh-ing song to-night!
got in-to a drift-ed bank, And we, we got up - sot.
hitch him to an o-pen sleigh! And crack, you'll take the lead.
Jingle, bells! Jingle, bells! Jingle all the way! Oh, what fun it is

to ride In a one-horse o-pen sleigh! one-horse o-pen sleigh!

Away in a Manger

Ascribed to Martin Luther

Carl Müller

A-way in a man-ger, no crib for a bed, The
The cat-tle are low-ing, the Ba-by a-wakes, But
Be near me, Lord Je-sus, I ask Thee to stay Close
lit-tle Lord Je-sus laid down His sweet head. The
lit-tle Lord Je-sus, no cry-ing He makes. I
by me for-ev-er, and love me, I pray. Bless
stars in the sky looked down where He lay, The
love Thee, Lord Je-sus, look down from the sky, And
all the dear chil-dren in Thy ten-der care, And
lit-tle Lord Je-sus, a-sleep on the hay.
stay by my cra-dle till morn-ing is nigh.
fit us for heav-en to live with Thee there.

There's a Song in the Air

Josiah G. Holland — Karl P. Harrington

There's a song in the air! There's a star in the sky!
There's a tu-mult of joy O'er the won-der-ful birth!
In the light of that star Lie the a-ges im-pearled;
We re-joice in the light And we ech-o the song
There's a moth-er's deep prayer And a ba-by's low cry!
For the Vir-gin's sweet boy Is the Lord of the earth.
And that song from a-far Has swept o-ver the world.
That comes down thru the night From the heav-en-ly throng;
And the star rains its fire while the beau-ti-ful sing,
Aye! the star rains its fire and the beau-ti-ful sing,
Ev-'ry hearth is a-flame, and the beau-ti-ful sing
Aye! we shout to the love-ly e-van-gel they bring,
For the man-ger of Beth-le-hem cra-dles a King.
For the man-ger of Beth-le-hem cra-dles a King.
In the homes of the na-tions that Je-sus is King.
And we greet in His cra-dle our Sa-viour and King.

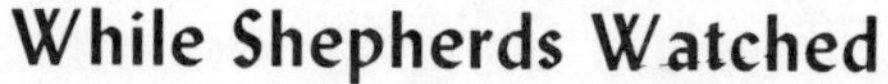

While Shepherds Watched

Nahum Tate

arr. from G. F. Handel

1. While — shep-herds watched their flocks by —

night, All — seat - ed on — the —

ground — The — an — gel — of the

Lord came down And — glo - ry shone a-

round, — And glo - ry shone a - round.

2. "Fear not," said he for mighty dread
Had seized their troubled minds.
"Glad tidings of great joy I bring,
To you and all mankind.

3. "To you in David's town this day,
Is born of David's line
The Savior, who is Christ the Lord,
And this shall be his sign.

4. "The heavenly Babe you there shall find,
To human view displayed,
All meanly wrapped in swathing bands
And in a manger laid."

We Wish You a Merry Christmas

Old English Carol

D7 G C
We wish you a mer - ry Christ - mas, We
A7 D +7 B
wish you a mer-ry Christ - mas, We wish you a mer-ry
Em +7 C +6 D7 D7 Chorus
Christ - mas and a hap - py New Year! Good
G D A7 D +7
ti - dings to you, And all of your kin, Good
G Am D7 G
ti - dings for Christ - mas and a hap - py New Year!

Hark! the Herald Angels Sing

Charles Wesley, 1739
Felix Mendelssohn, 1840
1. Hark! the her-ald an-gels sing Glo-ry to the new-born King;
2. Gra-cious bond of earth and sky, Born that man no more may die,
Peace on earth, and mer-cy mild, God and sin-ners re-con-ciled.
Born to raise the sons of earth, Born to give them sec-ond birth.
Joy-ful, all ye na-tions, rise, Join the tri-umph
Hail the heav'n-born Prince of Peace! Hail the Sun of
of the skies; With th'an-gel-ic hosts pro-claim,
Right-eous-ness! Light and life to all He brings,

Refrain
Christ is born in Beth-le-hem. Hark! the her-ald
Ris'n with heal-ing in His wings.
an-gels sing Glo-ry to the new-born King!
Sing Your Way Home
G G D7 D7
Sing your way home at the close of the day,
D7 D7 G C G G
Sing your way home, drive the sha-dows a-way. Smile ev-'ry
G G7 C C G
mile, for wher-ev-er you roam It will bright-en your road,
D D7 D7 G
rit.
It will light-en your load, If you sing your way home.

INDEX

TOPICAL INDEX

Action, Starters, Fellowship

Rounds

Graces

Children & Youth

Don't forget to sing Spirituals and Christmas songs with young people.

Camp Songs

Folk Songs

Morning & Evening

Newer Christian

Traditional Hymns

Patriotic

Spirituals

Christmas

Commitment